HUNTER TO THE DAWN

Happy Hunting!

HUNTER TO THE DAWN

by
Billy Ellis

Mississippi River Publishing Co.
Leland, Mississippi

The author gratefully acknowledges ***Poetry, A Magazine of Verse*** for permission to reprint, on page v., four lines from "Chief Capilano Greets His Namesake" by Constance Lindsay Skinner.

Photo credits. All hunting photographs were made by the author, except the following, which are printed by the permission of the photographer: pages 34, 199, 202, and color pages 3, 4, and 5 by Charlie Kroll; pages 33, 35, 65, 134, 138, 155, and color page 1 by Judd Cooney; page 104 by Flatiron Graphics; pages 168-169 by Gary Power; and page 37 by O. P. Williamson.

The illustration on page v is a stylized Haida halibut hook, NW Coast Indian culture, from the author's collection.

Artwork on page 2 by Bob Tompkins

Artwork on page 12 by Sam Beibers

LIBRARY OF CONGRESS CATALOGING IN PUBLICATION DATA IS AVAILABLE.
LC No. 88-13290
ISBN 0-9617591-3-5

Thou art come forth, as a hunter to the dawn,
Herding the antlered shadows down the forest slope.
Their swift fleeing hooves strike fire from the beaten sandshores of morning,
And the bright wraiths swoon upon the bright opening sea.

Northwest Coast Indian Song

DEDICATION

To my high school English teacher, Margie Riddle Bearss, who instilled in me a love for the printed word, even though she was unable to teach me to speak it properly;

To my mentor and companion of the Autumn trails, Charlie Kroll, a man who personifies the concept of "Fair Chase" and who encouraged me to write this book;

To my lifemate, Sally, who nurtures the cubs and keeps the den tidy while I'm afield;

To Fred Bear and Glen St. Charles, two names that will be breathed in reverence throughout the ages whenever Bowhunting is spoken;

To Bunky Wienke and Jim McCrory, who taught me how to bowhunt;

To Hugh Nichols, who sounded the horn of the big game hunter and set me on the high trails many years ago.

CONTENTS

PREFACE

I have known Billy Ellis for a number of years and can say without reservation that he is dedicated to the sport of archery, is a serious conservationist, and a tireless proponent of the cause of wildlife. This collection of his own stories of hunts, together with those of others' experiences, will serve as a worthy volume for outdoorsmen everywhere.

Billy's headquarters are his office at the Holmes County Bank and Trust in Lexington, Mississippi. His friends think of him as bank chairman, poet, and inordinate lover of nature. My daughter calls him "Precious Billy" in recognition of his generosity and congenial personality. Billy Ellis will be numbered among the forefathers of the champions of hunting who go into the next century as leaders in the field of conservation and guardians of wildlife.

Fred Bear

Fred, Billy, and Charlie

FOREWORD

I am honored to contribute to this *avant-propos* for my good friend Billy Ellis. Billy is a banker, and a good one. Now, bankers are often thought of as being rather "stuffy," but there is not an ounce of stuffiness in Billy. He is about as down-to-earth as bacon and eggs cooked over a campfire. And while of necessity he spends much of his time behind a desk, he is one who believes that Robert Louis Stevenson knew what he was talking about when he wrote: "It is not by any means certain that a man's business is the most important thing he has to do."

The growth of interest in archery in our country certainly is not altogether the result of fine tackle and precise shooting. Rather, it is due in large measure to the interest in ancient hunting rites, and to the tendency of the bow and arrow to kindle a spark long dormant in all of us and fan it into a flame which bursts forth in a finer sense of sportsmanship and conservation. The compulsion to hunt is a basic part of man's nature. When the tawny haze of autumn finds heavy-antlered bucks pawing scrapes on the edge of timbered coverts, when the great elk floats his eerie challenge on the mountain breeze, when the nomadic caribou begin their annual trek to wintering grounds, this urge—the legacy of our fur-clad ancestors—is irresistable.

There are bowmen who hunt with varying degrees of success in finding and getting game. Billy is one of the more successful at both. His unbounded enthusiasm and constant good humor in the face of adversity make him a desirable companion on any venture afield. And he writes with the same verve and excitability as he hunts. Always full-bore, that's Billy.

Like most serious bowhunters, he is deeply concerned for the welfare of all wildlife, whether game species or not, and for the preservation of their habitat. I know this, as Billy has faithfully and well served with me on the Pope and Young Club's Conservation Committee since its inception some years back. This is an organization which, for its size, has an enviable track record, having contributed, to the date of this writing, in excess of $50,000.00 to various federal and state level wildlife management and educational programs.

This collection of hunting tales, from both near and far, is basically meant to entertain and enthuse the sportsman. A taste of true adventure runs throughout, immersing the reader in the agonies and ecstasies of the chase. In reading it, however, one is also bound to absorb interesting information concerning the ways of the animals and the country they live in, and of what makes an avid bowhunter tick. The reader may also discover herein evidence that the real satisfaction of hunting lies in the seeking, the pleasure coming more from the process than from the product, and the best trophies being memories rather than the number or size of animals taken.

Billy and I are fortunate enough to be among those who have experienced one of life's greatest treasures—the joy of wandering through lonely lands with a trusty bow and true-flying shafts. May the Red gods grant us the time to share a few more wilderness campfires along the trail leading to the Happy Hunting Ground.

Charlie Kroll

INTRODUCTION

For the past twenty years, I have been blessed with the time, wherewithal, and some small ability to hunt the major big game species of North America with a bow and arrow. From time to time, a story of these exploits afield has made its way onto the pages of *Bow and Arrow Hunting*, *Bowhunter*, or *Archery World* magazines. This book is basically a compilation of those articles, and I am grateful to the editors for allowing me to republish them.

There are thirteen major species of big game trophy animals in North America recognized by Pope and Young and Boone and Crockett and currently allowed import status. They are Pronghorn, Cougar, Mule Deer, Whitetail Deer, Wapiti, Caribou, Moose, Musk Ox, Mountain Goat, Mountain Sheep, Grizzly Bear, Black Bear, and Bison. Jaguar and Polar Bear are not currently allowed import status. I have taken ten of the above species with a bow and three with a rifle. Along the way, I have also taken Spanish Goat, Corsican Ram, Black Buck Antelope, Mouflon Sheep, Wolf, Coyote, Javelina, Wild Hog, and three different subspecies of Caribou.

My quest has taken me to sub-zero polar regions, to scorching deserts, to great mountains with treacherous rock slides, to marshy tundras, and to sweltering swamps. It has all been wonderful! God's creation is so spectacular that it has to really be experienced to be believed. I am doubly blessed that I have seen it from horseback or on foot, and not from a train, bus, or car.

Other pearls of great price I have acquired along the trail are the most diverse and wonderful assemblage of friends and comrades that any man could ever hope for. They include world-class bow and gun hunters who are also professional and corporate giants, steel workers, riverboat hands, truckers, writers, doctors, farmers, etc. Others are my Indian buddies, some of whom cannot read or write, but can interpret signs of the passage of a bear or deer and feel the gentle stirrings of the earth—an art which we who are cooped up in boxes of concrete and steel have lost.

I am asked two questions more than any others.

The first: "When are you going to Kambia, Pambia, Yambia, or Ugandia?" (If these countries are not spelled right, stick around. They'll have a new name shortly, anyway.) To this question, I answer: "I have a friend (almost *had* a friend) Dr. Bob Speegle, who is a Weatherby award winner. Once while flying in a King Air across one of the above countries on safari, they were forced by weather and a petrol problem to detour to another third-world country. When they taxied up to the decrepit terminal building, they discerned the putrid smell of decaying human bodies. It seems that the local dictator, Broke-Assa, had just discovered how to rid his regime of student protest. He rid himself of students.

Through the swarms of flies came a host of beat-up jeeps filled with beaming, rum-filled natives toting mint-condition AK-47's who quickly surrounded the plane. When Bob tried to descend to terra firma, a swarthy camo-clad native with filed teeth got right up in his face. Bob was wearing a fabulous gold-encrusted lion's claw on a thick solid gold chain. The "soldier" grabbed the claw and chain in a ham-like fist, almost strangling Bob in the process.

"Like-ee! Like-ee!" he chortled through his pointed teeth.

"I like-ee you have! I like-ee you have!" agreed Bob, with mock ebullient good will. The grinning soldier then allowed Bob to undo the clasp without snatching it off his neck. A French soldier of fortune soon arrived and saved the day. The moral? 'Tis far better to give than to receive an AK-47 bullet.

That answers the first question.

The second: "In your opinion, which is the greatest game animal in North America?"

Without question, the prettiest is the jaguar; however, I will not hunt him until the import restrictions are lifted. The most underrated is the black bear. I have spent more time hunting him, with less results, than any other species. A really big whitetail deer is hard to beat, but my favorite trophy, and I think the most exciting animal in North America to hunt, is a magnificent bull elk.

We are now in the golden age of hunting in North America. More and bigger trophies are being taken each year thanks to outstanding game management, most of which is paid for by the hunters' dollars. *Vive la chasse,* but always remember to support wildlife conservation.

I relish the challenge of the bow, but I am not a purist. I enjoy hunting with either a recurve or a compound bow, and I occasionally get a kick (no pun intended) out of shotgunning or rifle hunting.

In this book, I have included articles about most of the major big game species that I have brought to bag, as well as a Mississippi wild hog story and a bow hunt in the Yukon that inadvertently turned into a gun hunt. The book also contains poems, ramblings, and tracks of a fellow traveler. You will also find a few tidbits of general hunting tips that you may or may not find useful.

This is not a basic "how to" book, however. This is a book that exudes the *joie de vivre* of hunting. May the Lord grant that I can trek the high trails for many seasons yet.

BILLY ELLIS
Choctaw Ridge Hunting Camp
near Possumneck, Mississippi

HUNTER TO THE DAWN

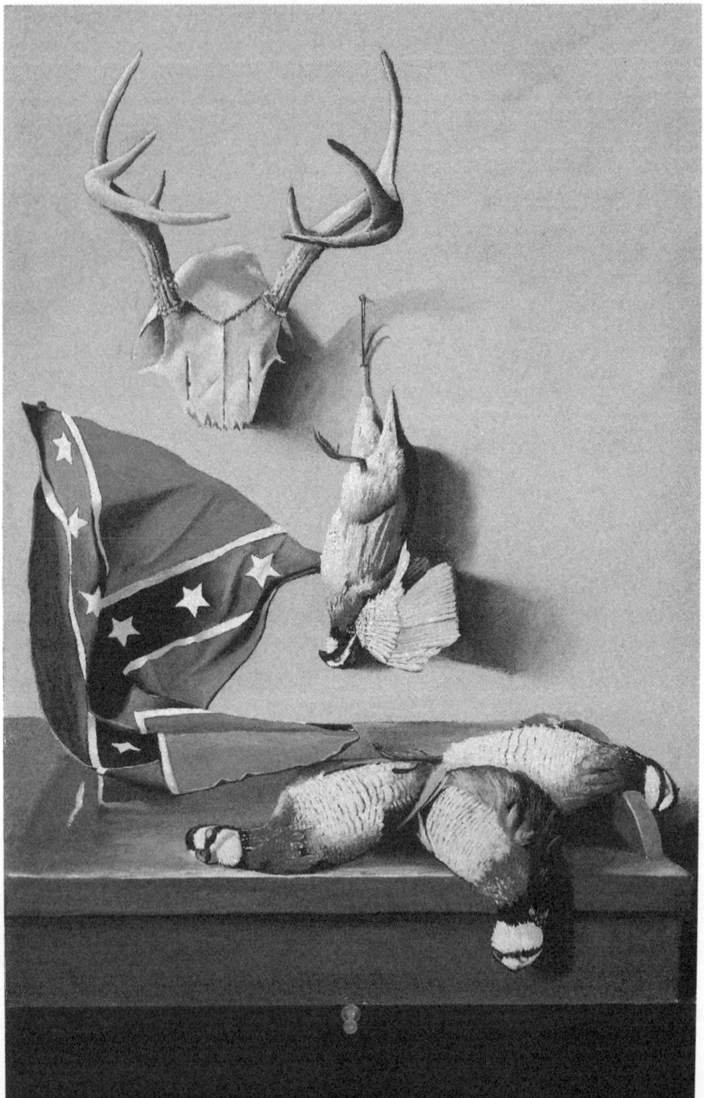

GENESIS

Noxubee Memories

The rooster crowed, the jackass brayed, and old Snaps, the pointer, bumped her rheumatoid backbone on the undercarriage of the creaking country house. It was a golden dawn in Noxubee County, Mississippi. The early-morning light refracted through the greying lead-glass panes, and now darkly through the misty memory of a grown man—then a touseled-headed city boy with a chunk of joy in his throat and the world before him.

I pulled on my clothes and made my way through the rambling, labyrinthine country house, out the never-locked back door, and onto the tin-roofed walkway to the old kitchen, which stood ten yards out back. I shivered in the morning cold until I pushed open the weather-beaten kitchen door. The heat inside warmed my body as well as my spirit. Granky, my Wilkins grandmother, held sway over the great wood stove, and her sons, recently spared from the Axis hordes, swilled

Granddaddy Wilkins and Snaps

great cups of strong coffee from ancient stoneware mugs. That smell of hickory smoke, coffee, and thick slabs of home-cured bacon is still fresh after forty years.

Once an old Eskimo woman, sick and depressed in a far and strange land, told her nurse, "Sometimes I raise my hands before my eyes and stare at them; right in my own hands I can see the shorelines, beaches, lakes, and mountains where I came from." In my heart's eye, when I see Granky's hands—plump, white, dishwater hands—kneading the dough, I remember where I came from. Those hands were once artist's hands at Mississippi State College for Women so very long ago, but she had given up art for a loftier and higher form of sculpture: kneading love into the dough.

The menfolk made plans for the day's hunt over an incredibly fine breakfast of grits, scrambled eggs, thick slabs of bacon, cat-head biscuits, and homemade fig preserves from the old fig tree behind the smokehouse. Thank goodness no one had yet discovered chloresterol, triglycerides, or carcenogens! We were in the best of times. Granky's boys were safe, and the world had a vibrancy and brilliance that only children can really feel.

The guineas were just starting their raucous cackling when Grandaddy Tyson Wilkins took me in tow. He and I would hunt the Back Forty. Old liver-marked Snaps ran by the smokehouse and headed out to "Quail Country." Grandaddy slipped three shells into his old beat-up Browning Sweet Sixteen, and we moved out past squealing pigs, pump house, horse barn, rusting harrows, and other extraneous refuse that always surrounds an old country homestead. The sun was just up and a thin fog still blanketed the gently rolling prairie hills. "Hup, Snaps!" Grandaddy called. The old pointer slowed and started to work, ranging back and forth, a flicker of white in and out of the patches of ground fog in the surreal early morning landscape. Then the white dot was stationary.

"She's got 'em!" whispered Grandaddy as I ran after him, panting and expectant, but not really knowing quite what to expect. He handed me the shotgun and whispered, "Shoot a bird, not the covey." I have never felt such responsibility except the time I shivered expectantly in a tiny church by the Mississippi River and said "I do."

Snaps had worked in tight on the covey in a perfect point. My heart was in overdrive. The sage crunched underfoot while I found the safety. "Walk past her," whispered Grandaddy.

An explosion occurred, and the buff bombshells rocketed out of the sage. I swung on the whole covey. Gun blast, kick, and no bird fell. I forgot to shoot again.

"We'll get the singles," promised Grandaddy. He then showed me how; with the pointer holding pretty, a single thundered up from underfoot, to explode in a shower of feathers. Old Snaps dutifully brought back each one, mouthing them gently, and we soon had six birds. Grandaddy called a rest break about noon.

We stopped at an old falling-down dogtrot house. The old man pulled a couple of roast beef sandwiches out of his hunting coat. "I'm feeling my seventy-four years," he confessed. "Let's sit here on the porch, and while we're here, I guess this is as good a time as any to tell you what tired really is and what courage is all about.

"My daddy, your great-grandaddy, had this farm and left me the big house. Some day in school, you'll learn in the history books about General Robert E. Lee and the Army of Northern Virginia. I don't know everything there is to know about all the battles, but I do know that Daddy was in our local company, the Prairie Guards, Company E of the Eleventh Mississippi Regiment in Lee's army. They were one of the first companies to volunteer, and since General Grant wasn't even a general then, much less raising havoc in Mississippi, Daddy's regiment was shipped to Virginia and fought under Lee for the whole war.

"He went through every battle that Lee fought, and was wounded seven times. It takes a heap of courage and a lot of love for your homeland to keep going when you're hurt, tired, sick, hungry, and thirsty most of the time. Both of his brothers, Henry Clay Wilkins and Davy Crockett Wilkins, were killed, one on either side of him, when they went up the hill in Pickett's Charge

Great-granddaddy Thomas Jefferson Wilkins and Great-grandmother

at Gettysburg. Out of the thirty-seven men in their company, only one man was able to answer roll call back down at the bottom of Cemetary Ridge that evening. Only one man, boy! I know folks in almost every house around here that grieved for a lost boy or two.

"Son, all day you've been complaining. Tired, thirsty, or something. I want you to remember what I just told you. Those boys went up that hill regardless of politics or ideology; they went up as simple country boys. They were defending what they perceived was right, protecting their homes and families, and they persevered through untold suffering.

"Right after Gettysburg, Daddy fought all the way back to Hatcher's Run right before Appomattox. By then, our troops were pitiful skeleton boys with no shoes and tattered, threadbare uniforms. They were starving and sick, but they still had that bright glint of bravery and total, even mystical, commitment in their eyes.

"On the last night, they were completely surrounded by the Yankees, and Lee's army was pushed up against a creek called Hatcher's Run. Just as the sun was setting for the last time on the greatest army the world has ever known, a long, rolling, shrill cry welled up. Starting three miles up Hatcher's Run and rolling down the Confederate lines, the Rebel Yell rolled like thunder down the creek, telling Grant that those lines were welded in a love that transcends any human comprehension.

"The next day, that bunch of pitiful scarecrow-boys was thrown into line. The tattered Stars and Bars flag fluttered before each regiment, only a few yards apart because each one had been decimated down to mere company size. General Lee and General Gordon rode the line, tears flowing down their cheeks. They knew the end was near, not just for the army, but for a way of life.

"General John B. Gordon stopped his prancing bay in front of a pitiful Confederate soldier. Both of his arms had been almost shot away, and they dangled helplessly at his sides. 'Get to the aid station, sir,' the general ordered. 'You cannot go into combat in your condition.'

"'I know I can't fight, sir,' the soldier replied, 'but I can still yell!' "

"'I CAN STILL YELL!' "

Lord, how I remembered that story. When the path grows dim, when the trail gets too rough, when the world closes in, I think of that pitiful, starving boy in homespun gray with the glint in his steel-blue eyes and a love that transcends all understanding in his heart.

Grandaddy pulled out an old, yellowed clipping from his pocket and handed it to me. "I thought you would like to have your great-grandaddy's eulogy, which was written by his commanding officer, Captain A. J. Ervin."

I started to read:

Eulogy of Thomas J. Wilkins, Co. E, 11th Mississippi Regiment:. . . . he was gallant and dependable in battle, and in camp and on the march he was always joyous and happy; never a cloud, however threatening, but that he could see the sunshine beyond. His most marked characteristic, however, was his intense and active interest in a sick or wounded comrade. No march could be so disagreeable and so protracted, no weather so severe as to prohibit his spending the night in a vigil by the pallet of a sick or suffering comrade; and he was one of the few who seemed to enjoy battling with death—in comforting where he could not cure; in soothing where he could not save.

Grandaddy and I left the old dogtrot house and walked back toward the big house. I didn't feel like hunting any more that day, and old Snaps seemed to sense it as she ambled along at feet all the way back to the house.

* * *

That was many years ago. The old house, called Sunnyside, is gone, a victim of the vicissitudes of time, and the cold, impersonal scalpel of a bulldozer blade. It's all gone—my tree house, the old smokehouse, the warm old kitchen, the feather beds, the old folks, the love and dreams that chink the walls of a country home. I go back occasionally, when the Lord calls another family soul back to the limestone clay of Noxubee County. As the preacher intones, "Dust unto dust, and to the dust returneth," my eyes stray to the large granite marker in our family plot. The inscription simply reads "T. J. Wilkins, Co. E, 11th Mississippi."

Bravery and love are all the consolation we need.

Dixie Eulogy

There is sadness in my Spring,
old man,

And the lonely plover
o'er silent water
re-echoes my loss.

No more the honeysuckle to weave
its melodies of gladness;
only now the warmth of my sadness.

As hand-in-hand no more,
down dusty Delta roads
with boyish dreams at twilight
and your rough laughter
in the air.

to W. R. Ellis, Sr.
A gentleman sportsman
and my "Big Daddy"

WILD HOG

Hound Dogs and Tush Hogs

The rich deep black alluvial soil which would grow cotton taller than the head of a man on a horse, already one jungle, one brake, one impassible density of brier and cane and vine interlocking the soar of gum and cypress and hickory and pinoak and ash, printed now by the tracks of unalien shapes—bear and deer and panthers and hogs and wolves and alligators and the myriad smaller beasts, and unalien men to name them, too, perhaps—in the trackless infested forest—

William Faulkner

The mist hung low over the fecund cotton fields in the Mississippi Delta and the rising sun cast a pink, hazy aura around the white cotton bolls. We wound ever further into the Yazoo River bottom land, dotted with oxbow lakes, bordered by giant cypress trees hung with Spanish moss. This was a land rich in song, story, and tradition. President Theodore Roosevelt once hunted bear here. William Faulkner set most of his hunting stories here. The Delta Blues were born here with such inspiring lyrics as "You got me way down here by de Rolling Fork/Treat me like a dog,/I gotta be here for the rest of my life/And all I did was shoot my wife!"

This was my home and stomping grounds and I was going hog hunting! Several weeks earlier, a friend of mine and hog man extraordinaire, Mike Braswell, had invited me to go. It took absolutely no arm-twisting, as I was already dying of anticipation. I was waiting for the whitetail bow season to open after a long, hot summer, and I wanted to bow hunt!

Mike had explained to me that several years before he had imported some wild Louisiana Piney Woods Rooters and had stocked them in a large, swampy tract of hardwood forest that ran parallel to a long ox-bow lake. The boars were large and had proved their irascibility by ripping up several of the local dogs who were unlucky enough to venture near. Now, Mike had as fine a pack of hog dogs as one could ask for. When I asked him once what breed the dogs were, he replied, "Catahoula Cur!" They looked to me like a cross between a Catahoula and a Plott hound, with something else mixed in that made 'em ugly to boot. But boy, could they hunt!

We pulled up to the edge of the woods and our team swung into action. Mike and his guide, Eddie Dixon, unloaded our fine cutting horses from the horse trailer, while my back-up gun, Sonny Russell, loaded up his trusty old "Thuddy-thuddy." The mosquitoes and horseflies were unbearable, so we sprayed each other down with insect repellent and quickly mounted up, then cast the pack of dogs. We were soon swallowed up by the almost impenetrable swamp. Sawbriers snagged our clothes and bare skin, and poison ivy and jagged limbs made the horseback ride uncomfortable, to say the least. We rode for at least a mile with no sound from the dogs. The rascals frolicked around us like toddlers at a Sunday School picnic. I was getting concerned and discouraged. Hog wallows and rooted-up areas were in abundance, but not hogs. Several of the dogs moved out of sight, and all of a sudden, a tremendous dog race blasted by us.

The hound music was just beautiful, and the sound rose and fell before finally disappearing into the distant woods. "Don't sound like a hog race," opined Mike. "Sounds like a deer race."

In a moment, all four of our dogs popped into view. "Astute observation!" I yelled to Mike, my disappointment thinly concealed. We rode in silence for another half-hour. I was thinking hog hunting must be like one writer explained combat duty: 95% boredom and 5% sheer excitement and terror. My buddy Sonny gave me a thumbs-down signal with a look of consternation.

That must have been a good luck signal instead, because up ahead, bedlam broke loose. Squalls, bawls, grunts, squeals, bays, and barks merged in a cacophony that would bring Spike Jones back to the land of the living. Then the hound music settled into a rhythmic cadence. "He's bayed!" yelled Mike, and we spurred our horses toward the sound.

I have bowhunted both black bear and mountain lion with hounds, and it is great sport, but once the animal is treed, and if you don't shoot your arrows away, the jig is usually up. Not necessarily so with ole *Sus scrofa*. He gives up very grudgingly. These babies have a look only a mother could love. They weigh up to 450 pounds, and are equipped with razor-sharp tusks that can, will, and have ripped dogs and hunters to bits. They have extremely thick hides and their shoulder area is virtually armor-plated. A sixty-pound bow is the minimum poundage I would recommend using for wild boar, and razor-sharp broadheads are a necessity. These beauties don't climb trees; they pick the worst thicket or brier patch in which to make their stand when bayed. They also have good eyesight and a keen nose, and upon seeing or smelling the approaching hunter, they usually either flee or charge.

The hounds were raising a clamor like a calypso band as we drew near. We quickly dismounted and tied the horses. Mike took the lead and, dodging briers and limbs, we closed the gap on the action.

The first thing I saw up ahead were the dogs. They were not lunging in trying to catch the boar, but were merely standing their ground and keeping up a steady clamor of barks and bays. Mike motioned me up and I saw why the dogs were so relunctant to fight. The ugliest, meanest, biggest hog that I have ever seen was glaring out from a thick blow-down at the base of a huge cypress tree. The cypress knees sticking up around the boar looked like tusks themselves.

I nocked an arrow and moved into shooting postion. I also looked around for a tree to climb. Then the boar spotted me.

He turned toward me, which is another problem because you can't take a frontal bow-shot. The front of the hog is like the front of a tiger tank. His beady little eyes caught mine. This thing could go either way. Then he bolted and ran.

A wild hog is not built like a domestic hog. A wild hog is rangier and has longer legs, and therefore is deceptively fast and agile. This hog ran over a knoll with the dogs in hot, vocal pursuit. I sprinted up the embankment. Down below a marvelous scene unfolded.

The huge tusker dodged left with the hounds close behind. He ran amuck in a muddy slough and tried to backtrack through the frenzied hounds. He started back toward me, then saw me and swerved to the right. My bow came up and I swung with the hog. The Thunderhead 125 was on its way. Arrow and hog almost merged, but then again, I *almost* bought McDonald's stock twenty years ago. The hog outran the arrow, and it plunked into the swampy goo.

The hog was tiring and bayed up again, this time in a thicket of ginseng bushes, the roots of which Orientals boil for an aphrodisiac. "I hope that hog hasn't been eating that stuff!" I thought with a shudder, easing in again, bow at the ready. The hog was popping his tusks like a bear. I could see great agitation among the bushes and a shot materializing. A dog ran in from the side and the hog spun to meet him. I had a fleeting lung-shot view and the arrow sped again.

"Thwak!" A high hit.

The hog dove over his dogged attacker, and, minutes later, bayed again some two hundred yards away. The sun had been up for some time, and it was as hot as a twelve-string blues guitar on a Saturday night. I was soaked in sweat and my glasses were totally fogged up. I wiped them off as best I could and continued to fight the muddy bogs, the bushes, and the briers.

The next Hog Alamo was worse than the other two. The bushes were over five feet tall and completely hid the hog and the dogs. I discerned the action below by the shaking of the tops of the weeds. The hog bayed up on a small island hummock a little way out from the lake bank. As I moved in on the hog, I was apprehensive. This was a perfect spot for a nest of water moccasins, there were no trees to climb, and the hog was wounded. It was spooky in there!

The hog's back suddenly appeared. I gapped down to where I thought his lung area should be and shot through the sawgrass. "Chunk!" A solid hit, and the hog bolted away. I was about to collapse, but ran again after the hog and the dogs. My old hunting buddy, Sonny Russell, who is pushing sixty years old, sprinted ahead of me in a rhino-like gait. He beat me to the action this time.

Author and his hard-earned tush hog

"He's down!" screamed Sonny, his adrenalin still pumping. Or had *he* eaten some ginseng?

The boar was truly awesome. 355 pounds of potential mayhem with long, razor-sharp tushes (as the tusks are sometimes called around here), malevolently red beady eyes, and rough, prickly hair on his upper back and neck made for a magnificent sight. His pelage was blue-grey with brown and black markings, which gave him perfect camouflage in his swampy habitat.

Sonny and I walked over to admire the downed tush-hog.

The animal struggled to its feet, teeth popping and neck ruff bristling. "Get back, babies! That thing'll kill you!" shouted Sonny. I quickly dispatched the boar, using two arrows to do the job. Sonny and I then sat down, drank gallons of water, and admired the beast.

The wild hog is truly a great trophy animal. It makes a wonderful mount, and is delicious table fare. Being a potentially dangerous animal, the boar adds another exciting dimension to a bowhunt.

"You know, Sonny," I ruminated, "the great bow-hunting writer-publisher, M. R. James, once wrote, 'the hunt's the thing!'"

Sonny slapped a giant mosquito and scratched his poison ivy rash. "You know, that may be true, but after all we was put through, I'm sho' glad that you're bringin' home the bacon, too!"

Sonny, Mike, and Eddie loading the wild hog for the trek out of the swamp

Rough Rider Legacy

"Far better it is to dare mighty things, to win glorious triumphs, even though checkered by failure, than to take rank with those poor spirits who neither enjoy much nor suffer much, because they live in the gray twilight that knows not victory nor defeat."

President Theodore Roosevelt
Founder of the Boone & Crockett Club

ELK

Wapiti Wonderland

"Eeeeeeoowww!"

No, that was not the sound of a bull elk bugling. It was my muffled scream as I fell headlong into the icy Colorado stream. My guide, Judd Cooney, had previously warned me of the slippery rocks, and now he surveyed me with a look of condescending sarcasm, as only a guide can do when his pilgrim hunter makes a stupid blunder.

I floundered up on the bank with badly bruised shin and ego. The icy Rocky Mountain wind hit my wet camo suit, but I dared not complain. I simply shivered in silence as we made our way down an elk trail paralleling the stream. On the mountain above, a bull elk suddenly screamed a challenge that was quickly answered by another bull from the willow grove in front of us.

"Let's try for the bull ahead," whispered Judd, picking a devil's snuff box from beside the trail. As he squeezed it, the brown powdery spores puffed out into the breeze. "The wind is just right for a stalk."

We sneaked near to the willows. The big 5 × 5 rack was thrashing a willow tree with a personal vengeance. Judd let me make the final stalk on my own. As I closed to within fifty yards of the bull, he sensed my movement and abruptly walked out into the open, standing broadside at thirty yards. He regarded me with a cold, red-eyed insolence.

My bow came up and the arrow closed the gap in a heartbeat, but it zipped an inch under the heart-lung area. The elk whirled and was gone in a flash. Because of the bull's size, in my excitement I had judged the distance at twenty instead of thirty yards. If looks could kill, ole Judd would have annihilated me at that moment. After a brief, stony silence, he muttered, "We'll get a bigger one soon." He obviously had more confidence in me than I had in myself right then, and we were soon on the prowl for elk again.

Another mile down the valley, I made a practice stalk on two rag-horn bulls. I actually got within good bow range before I backed off so as not to spook them.

This saga had all begun at the Pope and Young Convention in Bismark, North Dakota, some years back. I had overheard noted bowhunting guide Judd Cooney touting an outstanding elk area in the San Juan Mountains near Pagosa Springs, Colorado. At the time the 60,000-acre private ranch was not only known for its prime elk habitat, but it hadn't been legally hunted in over fifty years. Judd, who is a trained wildlife biologist, a former Colorado Fish and Game Warden, a noted guide, and an outstanding outdoor writer and photographer, was managing the ranch. I was the first and only bowhunter he would take that year. On advice from Harv Ebers, the Pope and Young membership chairman, I booked the hunt.

The months dragged by from April to September. I spent my spare time long-distance running and shooting my bow at targets up to fifty yards away. The West is big country, and the shots average longer out there than in the dense Mississippi riverbottom woods where I bowhunt for whitetails.

The great day finally arrived, and Judd picked me up at the Durango airport. He had done some pre-hunt scouting and assured me that big bulls were plentiful and in full rut. This all sounded too good to be true and did nothing to assuage my sleepless night.

Finally, Judd rousted me out of bed, long before daylight, and we were soon driving through the multi-padlocked ranch gate when Judd clicked on the spotlight. The illuminated scene around us almost made me blow breakfast. In every alfalfa meadow there were herd after herd of elk, and giant bulls were everywhere! I begged Judd to stop the truck then and there and let me hunt these elk after sun-up, but he just boomed his good-natured laugh and promised me more action in the high country.

He was true to his promise. After my blown shot and the practice stalk on the two immature bulls, we walked another mile down the valley and glassed the parks on the mountains above us. The horny monarchs were constantly bugling challenges to each other from mountaintop to mountaintop. Through my 7 × 26 Bushnell Custom Compacts, I soon located a fine five-point bull with his harem of cows in a park high above us.

Bull elk with his harem

"Want to go for him?" asked Judd.

"You bet!" I eagerly exclaimed, and we charged up a razorback ridge on an elk trail, concealed by the timber. When we got to within a hundred yards of the five-point bull, we sneaked to the edge of the timber to check him out. Just then, the sun broke over the rocky pinnacles of the San Juan peaks and illuminated him in a golden halo. I never saw a more beautiful sight. The bull would score well up in the book.

But he definitely wasn't in the bag yet. His harem was standing guard around him and getting within bow range would be difficult.

About that time, the bull took several steps our way and let out a tremendous bugle. He was immediately answered by a deep scream and raspy grunts from another bull in the draw right below us. Stunned, we dropped to the ground. Judd crawled over to the edge of the draw and looked down. He quickly motioned me over.

In the draw just below us was the bull of a lifetime! His giant 6 × 6 rack swirled from side to side like radar antenna. Every muscle in his huge body rippled as he moved, and the red eyes and the foam dripping from his mouth showed that the great beast definitely had plans for the smaller bull's harem of cows.

I quickly nocked an arrow in my sixty-three-pound Bear Alaskan and tried to pick a spot. Just as I was ready to release, the giant animal took a step forward and let out another bone-chilling scream. I was totally rattled, but somehow managed to make a smooth release. The arrow closed the distance in slow motion and plunked into the bull high in the mid-back area.

At the hit, the bull lunged uphill, and the other elk ran in all directions. The nice five-point almost ran over Judd. I simply collapsed on the ground from nervous exhaustion. When Judd came over and offered me a candy bar, my first bite included paper and all!

After a wait that seemed an eternity, Judd decided to go alone to look for a blood trail and come back for me when he found something positive. After a while, I eased up the ridge and saw Judd motioning for me to come down in the draw.

"See any blood?" I yelled.

"Don't see a drop anywhere," he replied.

My heart sank at that news, but I started walking his way. When I got close, I asked his opinion of the hit.

"It's a good thing you hit him good, or you might be dead yourself right now!" exclaimed Judd. He motioned for me to look down into a small ditch not fifteen feet below my boots.

There lay my monster bull, stone dead!

I let out a Rebel Yell that rocked the mountain, threw my bow high in the air, and scrambled down to examine the bull. My dream hunt was over!

After much jubilation and picture-taking, Judd pulled out a fifth of Jose Quervo and a film can full of salt that

The author approaching the downed trophy

he had cleverly concealed in his pack. We then toasted the majestic wapiti, the noblest stag of all. We wished aloud that his tribe might flourish and that his progeny might always roam wild and free in this glorious Wapiti Wonderland.

Proud author seated on the ultimate bowhunter's trophy—an outstanding Pope and Young elk

Wapiti Mystery

I wait in fog-clad eternity.
Far below his primordial scream
echoes up in sonorous majesty.

My body tenses as my trembling fist grips the bow.
In the ancient ghosts of fog-bourne rivers
I am born for this moment.

I hear the distant clash of his mighty antlers,
locked in gladiatorial combat with the saplings,
and sense the mystic urges of his harem
standing docile, but alert.

In his flaming moment, I stand to hear,
to feel his power,
and ponder my transience in his realm
of bent boughs and dew-dawn shade.

I am his dealer of death
with my small bow, in his moment of grandeur,
as his ghastly dirge blasts these stony peaks
like an ancient metaphor.

Down by the murmuring brook,
he drowns my soul in his madness
as I stand helpless and alone
on this ghostly morning.

My pulse is in my temples,
    in the blood-blown truth
        that blasts me from sensibility.

He is beyond life and love and death.
    He is the mountains and the aspens.
        He is with me in an atavistic brotherhood,
            but I cannot possess his spirit.

I will still his mighty bugle if it is willed.
    I'll claim him as a trophy if my puny arrow flies true.
        But he will always be the unattainable;
            with the mountain, the fog, and the silent stones.

BLACK BEAR

Desperation Bear

The shadows lengthened through the thick birch and spruce forest. A hint of breeze stirred the tops of the trees, casting eerily-moving shadows on the moss-carpeted floor of the deep Saskatchewan forest. Age-blackened stumps turned into bears that moved and stared at me as I perched high in my tree stand in a copse of birch trees.

"Snap!" No chipmunk or whiskey jay could break a limb like that! I gently eased my battered old Bear Grizzly II, which Fred Bear had signed and given me, off the bow hanger and ever so slowly turned toward the sound. With nerves as taut as my sixty-five-pound bow, I waited expectantly. Nothing. Was I mistaken? Could I have been hearing things?

Then, I heard an unmistakable sound of gentle pads stirring the leaves behind me. "Chip, chip." I craned my neck around and there, at seventy-five yards, was one of the finest trophy animals I have ever seen. A giant black bear, with nose testing the breeze, was staring a hole through me! His thick, lustrous fur gave him an almost mystical aura in the sunset-dappled shadows.

Downwind is not a good place for an animal to be, so with an almost haughty sneer, the bear swaggered off into the thick brush. This memory persists and I will always cherish it when my thoughts turn to super trophy animals. If I had been packing a rifle, he would have been paws-up.

I sometimes question the madness that grips bowhunters. Why do we do it? Is it really all that important to take an animal with a bow? I really can't adequately answer that question, but I still fondly recall the feeling that I had with my first bow kill down in the Mississippi River swamp when I hammered a fat whitetail doe with a puny arrow shot from an old Bear Kodiak Magnum recurve twenty years ago. I have been lucky enough to re-create that feeling of sublime excitement several times since then, and every time I do, I thank the Lord for the freedom to keep and bear arms that we enjoy, and for the beautiful game animals of North America.

This black bear hunt was especially meaningful to me. I had been invited to hunt with a friend, ace bowhunter Warren Buss of Fargo, North Dakota. Buss had phoned me three days before the hunt and informed me of a cancellation by one of his bowhunters. I had immediately cajoled my good friend, Sonny Russell, to accompany me on the hunt. Sonny is a dyed-in-the-wool rifleman and a crack shot. This would be his first big game hunt outside of Mississippi.

Warren Buss had made several successful black bear bowhunts to Saskatchewan and had four of the bears listed in the Pope and Young Club Record Book. The year before, Buss and Roger Rothaar had each taken a huge, 500-pound-plus bear with our guides, Randy Lorencz and Jerry Bien, who run Bear Paw Guiding Service at their camp south of Hudson Bay.

Lorencz and Bien are young, intelligent, and highly motivated black bear experts. They are both serious bowhunters, and huge Pope and Young-class bear trophies attest to their prowess with the old bent stick and string.

Our hunt logistics were nightmarish. We left Jackson, Mississippi, on Republic Airlines at 7:00 a.m. and, after two lay-overs, arrived in Fargo at 2:00 p.m. Buss picked us up at the airport and we joined the other two hunters in our party, Warren's son Daryl and Dick Wigdahl. The trip from Fargo to the bear camp had been in Buss's four-wheel-drive Chevrolet Suburban, pulling a trailer containing all our gear, plus a four-wheel and a three-wheel Honda ATM.

After a grueling fifteen-hour drive, we finally arrived at the camp, where we were housed in a rough but fairly comfortable cabin by the lake. We had delicious home-cooked meals at the Lamplighter Lodge, run by Roy and Cynthia Petrowicz. Cynthia's prowess in the kitchen was matched only by her wonderfully good-natured outlook on life. Joining us at the camp were two veteran bowhunters: Jim Miller, a PSE rep, and Steve Lepic. Both of these bowmen had many Pope and Young animals to their credit.

When we arrived on Friday, May 23, we were greeted by snow flurries, alternating with rain, and a freezing gale. Departing hunters, disgruntled by the foul weather that had ruined their hunt, still had high praises for their guides. They told us that our only hope for a successful hunt would depend on sunshine and no wind.

Black bear, aside from being omnivorous, have habits almost identical to the whitetail deer. They depend on their senses of smell and hearing, and will move little in a strong wind. Bear experts have written off a bear's eyesight as poor, but I have always felt that bears have adequate eyesight, and so try to keep my movements to a minimum when I am in a stand. The black bear, in my humble opinion, is one of the top bow trophies in North America, and I have hunted all thirteen major species now allowed importation and recognized for book entry by Pope and Young or Boone and Crockett clubs.

I have spent more hours afield hunting black bear with less results than any animal I have hunted to date. I have nine different species listed in Pope and Young or Boone and Crockett records, but still no black bear. This is good, because I can still continue my quest with unrequited gusto for a "giant, unobtainable *Ursus americanus*."

Our guides, Jerry and Randy, used meat scraps from packing plants, stale sweet rolls, and beaver carcasses obtained from trappers in the area as bait. Their baiting methods are similar to those practiced in the States. They use a fifty-five-gallon oil drum with two holes cut in the side, leaving one end closed and welding a door with a strong latch on the other. They stand the drum upright and pour the over-ripe bait into the can, then chain it to a tree. They didn't chain the drum on the first hunt, and the giant bear that I referred to earlier had picked up the barrel, bait and all, and hauled it two hundred yards out into the woods to rifle it at his leisure.

Bears love rotten beaver like kids love candy. A bait carcass was wired as high up on a tree trunk as a man standing on a three-wheeler can reach. My partner, Sonny,—who does not have a Ph.D. in English—requested no beaver bait near his stand. He explained: "Them beavers stink and has *magnets* crawling on 'em!"

Comfortable wooden tree stands were set up in birch trees within bow range of the bait station, and large logs were placed behind the barrels so that the bears would be forced to walk around in front.

The perfect set-up for arrow placement is when the bear is facing a quarter-turn away from you. You then do not run the chance that he will spot your draw. An arrow quartering in also has more chance of cutting lungs and other vital organs.

Guide Jerry Bien checking bait station

Sonny Russell in his tree stand

Although I will surely get some argument, I feel the best time to hunt bears is late in the afternoon. I have never seen a bear while early-morning hunting. I also feel that if you're hunting from the same stand day after day, it is a bad thing to be coming and going, making noise and leaving man-scent from dawn to dusk. The bears need a break, and so does the bowhunter.

I have hunted black bear with dogs several times, but I still prefer tree-stand hunting, over bait. The experience is close to hunting whitetails in a hot persimmon grove. In Saskatchewan, it was marvelous to be perched high in a birch tree as the sun slowly moved toward the western horizon. Hundreds of pairs of mating ducks whistled overhead, and their chatter and quacks gave me a slight pang for long-ago days of my youth, calling down the feathered ghosts into the flooded pin oak flats of the Yazoo River swamps.

Giant rafts of Canada geese flew by, "kee-lunk, kee-lunk"-ing their ancient navigation cries to each other. From nearby beaver ponds, came the lonely cry of a loon. Wolves howled and my work-a-day cares fell away. It was easy to see how Thoreau, Muir, Service, and Theodore Roosevelt lost their hearts to the wild and lonely places. Like them, I too, have been changed forever.

As my giant bruin lumbered away, the woods became deathly quiet. The small animals and an excited Mississippi bowhunter knew the predator was still around. Darkness fell all too soon.

I lowered my bow and nervously climbed down from my tree stand. It was a spooky quarter-mile walk back to my three- wheeler without my trusty Smith & Wesson .44 magnum at my side. All handguns are banned in Canada, a rule that I consider totally reprehensible.

Later, back at the trailhead, the hunters compared notes. Everyone had seen or heard bears except Sonny. "I heard a sound like a deer walking, but then a strange woodpecker started pecking from that direction," he explained.

"Bear clicking his teeth," opined the guides.

Sonny paled, grinned, and clammed up.

Our halcyon Canadian spring days were fleeing all too fast, but every one knows that time flies when you're having fun. Since Sunday hunting is not allowed in Saskatchewan, we had an all-day Sabbath bowhunting revival and fish fry on the grounds of the clubhouse. Joining us on the lake bank were ten fine Fargo bowhunters who were do-it-yourself bear-baiting ten miles north of our camp.

Sonny had failed to see a bear after three nights in the same stand. Although a good brown-colored bear was hitting the bait, it was obvious that it was feeding after dark. The guides decided to move Sonny to another stand where the bait was being "destroyed" every evening. Sonny tells his story:

"I was discouraged and tired. The 'skeeters and black gnats were eating me up. Aside from some strange woodpecker sounds, I hadn't seen a bear in three days of hunting. I was tired of sitting still and my rear and legs were cramped. I knew I was going to get skunked on this hunt.

"I was staring out at the woods past the bait when a movement a hundred yards out to my left caught my eye. A black patch of fur was moving through the thicket. It disappeared for a moment, but soon popped back into view. A black bear!

"I didn't know how big he was, but his body looked bigger than a deer, and that's the only big-game animal I had ever seen before this moment. 'He's big enough for me,' I thought. The bear then walked behind a Christmas tree and wouldn't come out. He finally stuck his head around the tree and sniffed the bait. 'Take one more step out from behind that Christmas tree and I'll show them guides some shooting!' I promised."

The bear complied, and Sonny took good aim at the sholder. His trusty 30.06 sent a 220-grain bullet through the bruin's boiler works, clipping all connections off the top of the heart. The bear collapsed and never moved. Russell had a beautifully-furred, fat and prime 260-pound sow!

From three miles away, I heard the barely-perceptible "pa-woom" of the rifle and hoped that Sonny had gotten his bear. All the other bowhunters were pulling for him, too. Right after the sound of the shot, I detected a movement out to my right.

"Ker-rash!" A big black bear blasted through the brush at full speed, breaking limbs, twigs, and bushes as it went. Then all went quiet.

"Ker-runch!" A much bigger bear came crashing by, hot on the first bear's trail. My heart was in my throat for several seconds. I tried to sort out what I had just seen. In retrospect, it seemed to me that the first bear was Pope and Young-class, and the second bear that chased him off was "Ol' Big 'Un" that I had seen the first night of the hunt.

Just as my pulse returned to normal, I heard a "wooof, click" behind a copse of spruce trees, just to the right of the bait drum fifty yards away. Shooting time was slipping fast. A great black shadow was ghosting up the main trail to the bait. The shadow had to be the monster bear. It moved like a musk ox, ponderous but sure-footed. It was coming in! My lifelong dream for a monster Pope and Young bear was coming true!

The bear took three more steps, stopped, sniffed, and rolled his massive head around, nose high. He didn't like the set-up. The old, well-developed instinct that had enabled him to become King of the Woods was still working for him. He turned to the right and walked behind the bait.

I could hear him breathing and snorting twenty yards away. He took several furtive steps and I finally could see his massive body behind the brush. Then I heard an agonizing sound—the "rummmmm" of a three-wheeler. As it got closer, the old bear simply vanished into the forest shadows, never to be seen again.

The three-wheeler roared up. "See anything?" called Randy.

"Yeah," I mumbled weakly, "I saw something."

Sonny with his trophy

"Sonny got a fine bear!" he exclaimed.

"I almost did, too," I thought to myself, climbing down. "Let's go see him," I said. We roared off, leaving my broken dream still a giant lumbering shadow in the twilight.

Sonny was ecstatic and he related his hunting story ten times before we got back to camp. All of us bow-hunters were delighted, for we are all brothers who hunt, whether we use a rifle or a bow.

In spite of all the action I had witnessed the first half of the hunt, I was lethargic and lackadaisical the next evening on the stand. I sat on my plastic milk crate and fought to stay awake. A bright sun was still shining at 7:30 p.m. The puffy cumulous clouds zipped overhead, pushed by a fierce gale, and the quickly-changing patterns of sun and shadow almost created flicker vertigo. In this state of ennui, I half-heartedly glanced up the hill a hundred yards to my left at one of my pet imitation bear stumps.

It moved! In fact, it started running down the hill toward the bait. Nothing will snap you back to reality like your quarry coming into bow range. Was it "Ol' Big 'Un?"

When it stopped briefly behind a stand of birches, I stood up and hugged the tree, then sneaked a peek. The bear had shrunk considerably from my first visual contact. In fact, it now became a grown but immature yearling. For a moment, I assumed the mother had already kicked it out to find a spring paramour, but a snapped twig behind the bait station changed that assumption. Lumbering straight in for the bait was one whale of a fine coal-black sow. She stopped behind the bait, sniffed and grunted. Satisfied with the set-up, she started around toward my tree, and looked straight up at me and my Adam's apple, which was going like a Larry Bird dribble. She gave a satisfied snort and walked toward the bait.

Junior raced over to the tree with the beaver carcass wired up high in it and scrambled up. The bear bit into the beaver, effortlessly crunching through bones, wire, and all. It was an awesome display. If a sub-adult bear could do this, think what Mamma could do to the beaver, or to me!

Ol' Mom soon felt that Junior just might eat up all her candy. She walked over, looked him in the eye, and made a deep rumbling noise in her chest. Junior got the message and retreated. Mamma lunged up the tree, mouth open, huge teeth bared. She grabbed the beaver's whole head in her mouth and crunched the skull into splinters. From eight feet in the air, she tried to jerk the head off the body, but it wouldn't budge. Finally, in an ingenious display of bear cunning, she chomped down on the beaver's head and released her grip on the tree with all four paws. With a sickening pop, the head pulled off the carcass from all the bear's weight. The bear fell butt-first, and hit the ground so hard I could actually feel the earth quake through the tree I was hugging—quite tightly, thank you.

I watched the bears until quitting time. When finally both were totally sated, they lay down like two fine old bear rugs on the ground near my stand. Then I heard "Ol' Big 'Un" "woof" out in the woods behind me. He wasn't about to try to run this really big old female off the bait!

I was in a quandry. I could beat my feet on the stand and shout to frighten off mother and son, but I didn't want any of the bears to equate that strange-looking platform and six-foot-tall quivering mass of protoplasm with a man. I still had three more days to hunt. I also didn't want Mamma to think I was an animated beaver carcass!

Time dragged by as the bears burped contentedly and I pondered my plight. Then I heard the throaty whine of Jerry's three-wheeler. "Good," I thought. "They are used to the comings and goings of their favorite maitre d'."

Jerry pulled up under the tree. The muffler was half blown out and the halogen headlights illuminated both bears. Instead of running off, they both walked in and out of the head light like other-world monsters from a sci-fi horror movie. "They'll run off now," I thought, as I climbed down and started to zip my bow into the bow case.

"Let's go!" screamed Jerry suddenly, as the bears made a tooth-popping mock charge. I must have looked like Roy Rogers making an over-the-rump mount on Trigger as I hit the vehicle's seat. We caroomed down the trail and completely disregarded the scratches we received from the thick briers and brush. I remembered with a shiver how the beaver carcass looked.

When I returned home, I would find out that bowhunter Mike Bowers of Albion, Michigan, who was hunting near us at about that same time, had been attacked by a mad old sow with two cubs. One of the cubs had begun climbing the tree where Bowers was sitting. Trying to scare the cub out of his tree, he had yelled and stomped on his tree stand.

"I heard the mother growl and she was on the way," he would report. "She came up that tree about ninety miles an hour. They can climb a tree about as fast as they can run on the ground."

Bowers had tried to climb higher up the tree. The bear had caught him about forty feet up, clamping onto his foot with her teeth. He would later tell us, "I'd kick her with one foot and she'd let go, then go for the other one." If she had kept hold of one foot, he believes the bear would probably have killed him.

When Bowers had tried to descend from the tree stand to retrieve his bow, the bear had charged up the tree again. After kicking her off his foot a second time, he had decided to stay put high above the tree stand. When he hadn't returned at the appointed time, his hunting buddy had come looking for him and had run the bears away.

Hearing this incident from Mike would give me an even greater respect for black bears, but meanwhile, my hunt was quickly drawing to a close. All of the hunters, except Sonny Russell, were developing furrowed brows, and the tension was becoming noticeable. Although our fine guides were doing all they could, the dastardly wind kept on at gale force. Jim Miller saw plenty of bears, but, like me, he was hoping his big one would come in. It didn't. Steve Lepic took a shot at a fine blond bear, but it was deflected by bone and the bear got away unhurt. Dick Wigdahl and Daryl Buss saw bears, but the wind had them spooked. And the wind blew Warren Buss's arrow askew and he nicked a bear in the foot. The bear barely flinched!

On the next-to-the-last night, as twilight deepened, a nice bear came in for me. Not "Ol' Big 'Un," but a good one. It tipped in, grabbed a bone, and ran. Ten minutes later, it slinked back in under the dark shadows of a spruce tree.

"This is it!" I thought. I rushed the shot, and the arrow zipped under a large bough of the tree. "Crunch!" came the sound of the broadhead hitting ribs and cartilage. The bear humped up, ran down the bear trail, and lay down. I knew I had my bear when I heard the "whoosh" of his last breath.

After a fitful night, our guide Jerry Bien, Warren Buss, and I went back at dawn to pick up my dead bear. When we walked over to the arrow, I couldn't believe what I saw. The arrow was totally devoid of blood and was sticking in a rotten log by the bait drum! The "crunch" had been the sound of the arrow hitting decayed wood, the "whoosh" a warning blow, and my bear was by then happily digging wild turnip roots.

What a disappointment! The old skunk fever was setting in. That afternoon was our last to hunt. I went back to camp and took a three-hour nap. The guides had a wonderful bear-meat barbeque, which was delicious and the fellowship was fun, but I did not participate; I was thinking bear.

When the afternoon hunt-time arrived, I was well rested and calm and I was going to make a bowhunt out of the situation. I got up in my stand for the last time. I couldn't sit down. Mosquitoes and blackflies buzzed around the inside of my glasses like some exquisite Manchu torture, but I still didn't move. My feet hurt, my legs ached, and the sun was imperceptibly but definitely going down. I put the farmer's crisis, unemployment rates, the Canadian timber glut, and all other worries from my mind. I was thinking bear!

The final countdown of the hunt began when I heard a slight rustle behind the bait set-up. A long yellow nose poked around a log and a really fine, beautifully furred, coal-black bear sauntered into view.

No hesitation this time. This was it, the moment of truth was here! My old faithful Grizzly II came quietly off the bow hanger. The bear turned sideways and sniffed a meat scrap. I took a deliberate sight picture on a spot right behind the bear's foreleg and my Easton XX75–2114 arrow tipped with a Thunderhead 160 disappeared into the bear. Or so I thought.

"Thunk!" came the sound of an arrow hitting a solid log. The bear went from sitting still to out of sight, instantly. "I missed that damn bear and hit a log again," I thought. "The hunt's over!"

Ten seconds later, I heard the most chilling sound that a hunter can hear: an "urrunk, urrunk" from the very soul of the bear. Then all was still. Was it a death moan?

Then the bear fever hit. I tried to hang the bow back up, but I was shaking too hard. I tried to get a fresh dip of snuff, but I couldn't get the can out of my pocket. Finally, I just sat down on the milk crate for the last time. After fifteen minutes, I lowered my bow to the ground and climbed down behind it.

Lord, I hated to go look for that arrow! The twenty yards to that log were the longest yards that I've ever walked. When I finally saw the arrow, it was covered with pink, frothy lung blood! I couldn't believe it! Especially after my *faux pas* of the day before. I took out a kleenex and wiped it on the arrow. I had to get a second opinion.

I fairly floated up the hill to my three-wheeled Honda. Warren Buss soon pulled up, and I showed him the evidence. He concurred with my verdict and roared away to get the guides. Thirty minutes later, he returned with Jerry, and we looked for a blood trail. We found nothing.

Flashlight in hand and growing desperate, I plunged down a bear trail in hopes of spotting the dead bear.

The trail led down into a thick hollow. I shined the flashlight under the overhanging branches of spruce trees. Bones and hollow-eyed skulls grinned back at me. Bear tracks and bear droppings were everywhere. I felt like I was in some B-grade Dungeons and Dragons movie set. The night was pitch-black, but I had to find that bear.

I crossed a new bear trail. It led to the left and back up the hill to the bait. I started up the hill and, as I topped out, I found myself eyeball-to-eyeball with a bear!

I opened my mouth, but no sound came out. The bear's eyes were glazed over. I had my desperation bear!

I called for Warren and Jerry and admired my trophy. It was a prime, beautifully-furred, 300-pound, coal black bear. Not "Ol' Big 'Un," but a heck of a consolation prize!

The author and the Desperation Bear

MULE DEER

The Luck of Orion

The two magnificent mule deer slowly grazed up the mountain in the fading Colorado twilight. They finally paused, turned their huge Pope and Young-class racks to the left, and spotted us. With majestic disdain, they slowly trotted uphill and disappeared into the quaking aspens. The eleven Mississippi bowhunters who rimmed the canyon had trembling hands and pounding hearts as they returned to camp that night.

This incident occurred during our scouting hike on the afternoon before the opening of the Colorado bow season. We were guests of outfitter Doug King at his beautiful ranch on the Uncompahgre Plateau near Grand Junction, Colorado. King runs a top quality hunt on his family ranch, with additional acreage leased to give him a total of 20,000 acres of prime mule deer territory. The terrain, at 8,000 feet elevation, is covered with aspen, scrub oak, and sage, and dotted with springs and beautiful beaver ponds. King is a mule deer expert who works his tail off for his hunters, all of whom were destined to get shots at bucks on this hunt.

As we pulled into camp that first night, the twinkling stars of the constellation Orion the Hunter lit up the eastern sky. I made a silent wish to the hunter's stars, as I'm sure bowmen have done through the ages, and felt the same atavistic excitement and anticipation of the quest that our Indian brothers must have felt when they hunted these same mountains with the bow and arrow hundreds of years ago.

None of our hunting party slept soundly that night as visions of Pope and Young-class bucks shaped our dreams, and at five a.m. we all bounced out into the crisp, cool dawn, ready for the big day. This particular morning, our group would be in blocking positions for a drive made up of ten bowhunters from the adjoining ranch. We were to line a ridge overlooking an aspen draw. As our pickups slowed to let the first hunter out, five huge bucks ran in front of the trucks, not twenty yars away. In their excitement, they then jumped back across the road and ran down the mountain into the quakie draw in front of our stands.

What a way to start the first drive! We were really fired up, and the morning was quiet for a short time after everyone took their assigned stands along the ridge. After about ten minutes, I detected movement along the western horizon. Five huge bucks, probably the ones we had seen earlier, materialized like ghosts in the early morning mist and headed for the draw right in front of us. Every stander on the ridge was having heart flutters as he silently prayed that the bucks would head his way.

This, however, was not to be. The bucks milled around for a few minutes and wisely sneaked out of the bottom of the draw.

A couple of standers to my left thought that the drive was over and walked out into the open to talk. At that moment, another big buck topped the ridge and headed straight for them. The two talkative hunters were struck dumb, but quickly recovered, filling the air with arrows and oaths as the giant critter headed for the rising sun in that unmistakable muley bounce.

While I was distracted by this action, intuition told me to recheck the far ridge in front of me. I quickly spotted a hint of movement and could barely make out two widely-spaced antler tips coming up over the ridge. The buck's rack just kept on coming up for what seemed like an eternity while I gasped in wonder. This was the highest-racked muley that I had ever seen, and a sure candidate for the book.

He topped the ridge and bounded straight for my position. Instead of sneaking out of the draw like the other bucks had done, this one barreled on through and headed straight for me. When he was fifty yards out, I crouched low in the scrub oak and came to full draw with my Bear Alaskan compound. The hoofbeats were now merging with my heartbeat. Suddenly he materialized, in all his glory, his huge velvet-covered rack thrown back as he sensed danger.

There was no time to admire him now, however.

Dr. Andy Reese, Nicky Nichols, outfitter Doug King, Bunky Wienke, and guide Dale Kelly

Man's inborn hunting instinct culminated in me at that moment as I automatically placed my sight pin on his heart-lung area and released. The 2114 Easton aluminum arrow hit the right spot with a loud "whack!" and the monster whirled away like a runaway horse.

I immediately ran over a little rise to try to keep the deer in sight and was delighted to see it slow up and bed down two hundred yards away. I stalked to within seventy-five yards of the bedded deer, and all I could see were the huge antlers slowly turning above the sage like a radar antenna as he searched for further danger. I was hoping that this buck would expire in his bed, but some of the drivers pushed through and unintentionally moved it out.

It was clearly time to call an expert, so I quickly located my guide, Art Cook. Art is one of the most knowledgeable mule deer bowhunters in the country, with several muleys near the top of the record book. He immediately took the situation in hand and sent the majority of the hunters on another drive, organizing the best trackers to help us.

As we topped the next ridge on a decent blood trail, Art motioned me up to him. "Nock an arrow," he whispered. My heart did a double flip, and I did as I was told. He pointed down the ridge. Lying across a trail was a huge antler.

The closer I got to the deer, the more excited I got. There he lay, in all his regal splendor. The Savora Super S broadhead had traveled through both lungs and had taken its toll on this magnificent creature. I stood there in reverence and awe of my first Pope and Young record animal. There are few feelings any finer.

The buck was the largest three-pointer (Western count) to make the Pope and Young record book. Scoring 161-2/8, it had a right beam length of 24-6/8", a left beam length of 23-5/8", and an inside spread of 20-4/8". The tines were, obviously, incedibly long.

That night the bright stars of Orion the Hunter still shined down on our camp. Although I claim not to be superstitious, I murmured "Thanks for the hunter's luck, Orion" before the coyotes' song lulled me to sleep.

Author with his Luck of Orion trophy

Athabascan buddies

Paean to Alaska

Float me somewhere down the Kuskokwim
   where the best is like the worst,

And there ain't no T.V. preachers,
   and a man can slake a thirst.

Just to stalk the host of caribou,
   that wander o're the plain,

And let their great unfettered freedom
   strike my regimented chains.

With my Athabascan buddies,
   that's where I long to be,

On the barrens of Mulchatna,
   that call enchantingly.

The Barrens of Mulchatna

MOOSE

Moose of the Yukon

The Yukon! The very sound conjures up thoughts of a strange and far-off land, a starkly beautiful landscape, forbidden and remote. It speaks of lonely, blizzard-filled nights, of forgotten miners frozen in their cabins with large gold nuggets still clutched in their gnarled hands.

As the plane dropped down over Chilkoot Pass, where the miners faced death and hardship during the gold rush, I saw a sprinkling of the gold of the Arctic birch on the mountainsides. After a brief stop in Whitehorse, I was off again on a rickety but reliable DC-3 bound for Mayo, the last jumping-off point in the northern Yukon. I stayed overnight in this town of dirt streets, sled dogs, and friendly inhabitants before I was picked up by my outfitter, Don Marino, and his lovely bride Dawn the next morning.

Soon we were roaring down the Mayo River in a single engine DeHavilland Beaver. Our pilot, W. A.

Crossing Bonnet Plume Lake with the trophy moose, in the teeth of a fierce Yukon blizzard

Hayworth, looked anxiously down at the pontoons, but they refused to break the surface of the water as we were at full gross load. We were headed toward the bank at a bend of the river, and I was subconsciously pulling up on the co-pilot's seat, trying to lift the plane into the air. At the last moment, we careened around the bend, and the plane wobbled into the sun-bright sky.

We were 130 miles outbound for Bonnet Plume Lake to make a rendezvous with a moose, and after viewing some incredibly beautiful scenery and an occasional Dall sheep on the lonely mountaintops, we began our descent. Bonnet Plume Lake reposed like an azure jewel between the snow-capped mountains. As we taxied up to the wharf, I was delighted to find a comfortable camp with a log storage cabin, plywood cook house, and three tents with plywood floors and sides.

At the Spokane Pope and Young club the preceeding Spring, Jack Williams, a fine bowhunter, had overheard me express my desire for a good bull moose. Four months later he had phoned to inform me that a hard-working young outfitter named Don Marino had a last-minute opening for a moose hunt and wanted to take a bowhunter. That settled it; I had to go! I immediately started shooting my bow in earnest and jogging a mile a day. The pounds and days fell away, and at last I was here in this beautiful place.

Of the 27,000 residents of the Yukon, 15,000 live in Whitehorse. This desolate expanse holds excellent game populations with low hunting pressure. The Yukon wilderness encompasses 207,000 square miles, and Marino's leased hunting area contained almost 5,000 of them. The Bonnet Plume drainage is a natural gathering place for rutting moose that migrate looking for cows when the snows hit the high country around it. Marino's area also abounds with bear, caribou, and sheep. A gun hunter had scored on a forty-two-inch Dall at the Goz Lake sheep camp shortly before I arrived.

The Yukon is a land of paradoxes. You can't find a bottle of Yukon Jack, but they sell Southern Comfort. The people are hospitable, the fall weather is not. A hunter must be prepared for anything the clouds dish out. On one particular day, it rained and then snowed, and then the sun came out. The temperature the last week in September can range from fifteen to fifty-five degrees, so a hunter must dress in layers. A top-quality rain suit and a warm jacket are musts. I had good luck with the new Doughtery Thinsulate bowhunter jacket on the really cold days.

Although most guides don't wear camo clothes, I think they are important for a bowhunter. I also prefer warm, water-repellant mittens instead of gloves, and I take plenty of corn pads and antibiotic salve. For footwear, I had good results with a pair of L. L. Bean rubber-bottomed shoe pacs and a pair of Browning Highland featherweight boots with cleated soles. Those long stalks can be murder on your heels!

A bowhunter should carry the heaviest bow he can

accurately shoot. I used a Bear Grizzly II set at sixty-three pounds and shot Dougherty Smokes in 2117—vanes are a must—and tipped the arrows with Razor-back 4's.

The first morning of the hunt, Marino and I started out climbing the mountain behind camp. The scenery was spectacular, but the going was rough through the tag alder and shintangle. We finally made the top and backed against a shale outcrop to glass down into a moose meadow. After about twenty minutes, Marino stood up and immediately dropped back down to the ground.

"Big grizzly!" he whispered excitedly.

I glanced over the granite lip, and there below me at one hundred yards was a beautiful chocolate bear placidly munching blueberries. I stuck my shooting hand under my left arm to warm it up. We began to stalk.

At sixty-five yards, the big bear stared a hole in us; we froze on the mountainside. When he resumed his culinary quest, we again started to close the distance. An errant wind draft hit the backs of our necks, and, without looking back, the bear hit a full, rolling gait down the mountain. When he came into full view, we could see that he was a huge chocolate-phase *black* bear, not a grizzly. It had still been a throat-tightening, although marvelous, experience.

The rain soon began in earnest, and I was quickly drenched. I have a theory that rain doesn't freeze at thirty-two degrees in the Yukon. The water trickling down my neck had to be ten degrees, and only the ancient crags knew the exact wind-chill factor of the Arctic wind. I told Marino, "I can't even feel my bowstring, much less pull it back!"

He laughed. "I can't even blow my nose!"

Without another exchange, we headed back to camp. Dawn must have sensed our approach, for she had steaming cups of hot chocolate laced with Southern Comfort and a wonderful gingerbread cake waiting for us in the warm cook house. Nothing has ever tasted better!

The next day was my big one. It began with a fine breakfast of caribou tenderloin, fried in spices and butter, with eggs and all the trimmings. At first light, we paddled the canoe to the far east end of the lake, then trudged up through the tricky muskeg and alders, and finally hit the bare, tundra-covered mountains. After an hour of concentrated glassing of all the mountains and muskeg bottoms in view, I was sweeping my binoculars across the far mountain for the second time when the flash of a tiny white speck caught my attention. When a small black object materialized under it, I cried, "Moose!"

Marino soon had the forty-power Bushnell spotting scope fixed on the distant animal. "Very nice!" he exclaimed.

We spent the next hour in constant visual contact with the animal as he meandered several miles across the timberline meadows. He finally bedded down at the foot of a huge shale slide that pointed down to him like a giant arrow. We had a decision to make.

"He's a long way off," Marino declared.

"Let's go for him!" I exclaimed.

We quickly made our plans. We couldn't cross the marshy muskeg or the raging river between our mountain and the moose's on foot, so we decided that Marino would hike back and get the canoe while I angled down to the river, and he would pick me up.

We both fairly floated down the mountain like Tibetan Long Gom air walkers. We met at the river and had a rough time shooting the rapids, but soon beached the canoe and hit the ground running. After traveling through some of the worst muskeg and alder thickets I have ever fought through, we broke out above the timberline miles later, with blistered heels and searing lungs. We rested, ate a quick lunch, and were ready for the final act in this exciting drama.

The wind was in our favor for the stalk. We had been out of visual contact with the moose for two and a half hours. Was he still bedded down, or had he moved left, right, or toward us? When we had last seen him, it looked like he was standing in knee-high brush. We found out it was head-high on us. Moose are big animals.

We quietly and carefully made our way up a babbling brook toward the shale slide. The suspense was nerve-shattering. Two steps, stop. Three steps, stop. Suddenly, "Down!" Marino exclaimed. We flattened ourselves against the high bank of the brook in the tag alders. "He's right ahead of us and coming our way!"

I saw a sight I'll never forget. The giant walked over to a large willow tree and absolutely destroyed it with several swipes of his huge rack. Sharing the same piece of real estate with a horny and irate monster while holding only a bent stick in my hand is my idea of sheer ecstasy! The big bull then turned and started my way, his rack ranging high over his head like a radar dish. His neck was swollen in the rut, and he was sounding "euuunh, euuunh," with each step. When his head went briefly behind a spruce tree, I jumped behind a bush near the bottom of the brook.

He was sixty yards away, then fifty. Every muscle in his huge body showed in high relief. My blood pressure had to be nearing a critical point. When he was thirty-eight yards away and still walking and grunting, my bow came up. The sight picture looked good, and the arrow was on its deadly way. It hit with a "thunk!" high in the lung area.

The beast took off like a runaway Mack truck down the mountain, crashing through trees and brush and dislodging boulder-sized rocks. When the noise quieted down, jubilation reigned, and Marino and I pounded each other and danced around until we fell off into the creek. Then began the awful anticipatory wait that only a bowhunter can know. The hit looked good, but how good was it?

After twenty minutes we began the process of following the tracks. Not one drop of blood could we find. We moved apart to cover more ground as several other trails converged. Three hundred yards down the mountain, Marino shouted.

We both dove for the moose, which lay stone dead in a lovely mountain glade. He had gone in on his nose, knocking down saplings and scooping up tundra moss in his two front shovels. The size of the critter was staggering. He was elegant and impressive even in death.

After some whooping and back-slapping, the real work of cleaning him began. We found that the arrow

Outfitter Don Marino and the author with moose

had taken him through both lungs. Three hours later, we headed back to camp with the tongue, rack, and cape. We had a real celebration when we ate the delicious boiled moose tongue that night, relieved that the hunt was over.

"That stalk wasn't tough unless your socks turned red!" Marino informed me.

"It was, and they did!" I groaned as I dabbed more salve on my raw heels.

The next several days were spent hauling the moose meat back to camp and fleshing the cape and skull cap. There was also some time to hunt caribou and grizzly, which was enjoyable, but the animals and the weather refused to cooperate. We were caught in a fierce blizzard on a bare mountainside one day and had a tough time getting back to camp. This incident only heightened my appreciation of the hunt. Since the weather was deteriorating, we called in the float plane for my trip out the next day.

As the spectacular vista of the snow-capped Selwyn mountains unfolded below the plane on the trip back to Mayo, I had time to reflect on the total hunt experience. As in Oscar Wilde's "Ballad of Reading Gaol," another paradox arose: I loved this giant moose, but I had killed him. He is now memorialized in taxidermy, however, and will be stamped in my memory forever, along with the snow-capped peak that rose above him in that lonely glade with the babbling brook, the bitter wind, and the raven's cry.

The author packing out his magnificent moose antlers

CARIBOU

Tuktu, Brother to the Wind

In the eye socket
of a caribou skull,
A tiny crowberry
makes its statement.

A letter arrived on my desk that spring day. It read, in part, "Sharpen your broadheads, file your teeth, and re-pad your trusses, for this Great Caribou Culling Expedition will boggle the mind and beggar the imagination!" It was signed by Charging Gopher, alias Charlie Kroll, bowhunter extraordinaire.

However, just getting to the hunt was adventure enough!

We arrived at the jetport in Shefferville, one of the most northerly outposts in Quebec, for the final leg of our flight, which would be 200 miles north to the camp. We then boarded a Laurentin Air Service De-Havilland Otter float plane and settled back. However, after an interminable warm-up cruise around the lake, our pilot's radioed intent to take off drew a "return to base" order. A fog bank had moved in from Labrador and had reduced visibility to zero at our intended camp site. We were then driven back to town.

Finding no vacancy at the local hotel, we were taken to a dilapidated mobile home left vacant by a miner. There we met the other three members of our hunting party. The three rifle hunters from upstate New York, added to our six bowhunters (Jim McCrory and I from Mississippi, Jim Dougherty from Oklahoma, Paul Brunner from Montana, Charlie Kroll from Florida, and Lee Kline from Colorado), presented a puzzle. We all tried to figure out how nine people could sleep on three single beds with linen partially digested by a diligent colony of bedbugs.

After a long search, we found a suitable camphouse on a lake near town. McCrory stayed outside to enjoy the scenery too long and came in to find only a broken folding cot with too little cover. His cot also tended to collapse every time he turned over, and he walked like a crab the next day until his muscles returned to normal.

The weather cleared the next morning. We took off past a cross standing on a small island in the lake, and I made the serious mistake of asking the pilot why it was there. "One of our planes with all hunters aboard 'bought the farm' down there last year," he explained.

I swallowed hard and tried to enjoy the panorama of the vast and desolate tundra that unfolded below us.

"This reminds me of a book I just finished reading about a family that was stranded in this country many years ago," Charlie mused.

"They finally got out O.K., didn't they?" I asked.

"Of course not! They found the diary with the bodies five years later," Charlie answered.

I quickly scanned the plane for survival gear but saw only a tiny first aid kit. "Let's look for caribou," I suggested.

An anxious hour later, our floats touched the beautiful George River. While we waited for our guides to take us out from Twin River Lodge, someone shouted "Bulls in the river!" As we watched, two giant bulls leisurely sauntered out of the water and walked up and down the opposite shore. That got us going, even though they had disappeared by the time we were assigned a guide.

Lee Kline and I were to hike through the high granite-topped mountains behind camp, do some scouting and, hopefully, some stalking. Our assigned guide was Isadore Belvin, a wilderness-wise Cree Indian. We worked in a large circle through the mountains, enjoying the hike in the cold Arctic air and glassing several fine bulls, all of which proved untakeable due to water and other topographical barriers.

Late in the afternoon, we decided to take a breather and guard a caribou trail coming down from a high ridge and leading into the George River. We each took separate stands about 200 yards apart. I was glassing some caribou skylined behind me when I heard a whistle. I glassed across the river, where McCrory and Dougherty were madly gesturing my way.

I nocked an arrow, eased up from behind a small bush, and looked behind me. Coming down a caribou trail straight for me was a huge black bear. Bears were

Bowhunting great Charlie Kroll and author glassing for George River caribou

protected in this area, but I wondered if bowhunters were equally protected from bears. My heart stopped when the beast reared up on its hind legs at nine steps and sniffed and snorted. I was at full draw and my top pin was aimed dead at its chest. Many things crossed my mind before the bear finally dropped to all fours and ambled off, showing no more fear of me than I would of a chipmunk.

That night, after a fine dinner with wine accompaniment, I was officially christened in honor of my experience. I had hoped they would honor me with "Standing Bear," but Dougherty talked them into "Bear Stool" instead. That's the medical term rather than the bar term, but at least it was better than some other suggestions.

The second day was McCrory's and Brunner's. Dougherty, McCrory, and their guide, Bernard Costill, took a motor-powered freight canoe up the George River. The weather was clear and cool, a beautiful day to hunt. Their guide took them to the top of a mountain on the east side of the river. They could see the surrounding area for miles around, with a good view of the George River to the west and the Dupas River to the south where it empties into the George.

They saw several caribou in the mountains, but their attention was drawn back to the George River. McCrory had noticed the first day that the caribou were traveling east to west, and that as the trails came out of the mountains, they seemed to merge near the river. The caribou, upon swimming to the west bank, would emerge, shake off the water, then generally walk parallel to the river before starting up the mountain. "That's where I need to be, where the caribou parallel the river," he had decided.

His thoughts were confirmed as six huge bulls walked the shoreline while the hunters watched from the mountain. Dougherty agreed with him, so they went back down, crossed the river to the west bank, and began building a blind at a point where the bulls had been. McCrory and his guide located the blind in the willows away from the water's edge where any animal approaching would pass within twenty-five yards of the blind. Dougherty walked upriver to another crossing. In less than an hour, six cows and calves and two bulls walked past, but the bulls weren't big enough, so McCrory shot them with just his camera.

It began to rain. As McCrory adjusted his raingear, his guide told him, "Big bull in the river." One of the two bulls had large antlers, wide palms on top with long tines. The bez points were extended out to near the end of his nose. They came ashore and headed toward McCrory.

One hundred fifty yards away, they disappeared behind a bend in the river. McCrory could only sit there and sweat until the bulls reappeared directly in front of his blind. To get ready, he removed his raincoat and jacket and shook as much water from his bow and arrows as he could. "Plastic fletching was good to have then," he would later say.

After what seemed an eternity of waiting, he heard

HUNTER TO THE DAWN

the clicking sound of approaching caribou hooves. He reminded himself that he must let both bulls pass in full view so he would be sure not to shoot the smaller bull.

"I was intently following the sound of the hooves when a huge set of antlers appeared," McCrory said later. "It was him! The big boy was in the lead, but at that instant he stopped and looked in our direction. My heart hit bottom. The bull was suspicious. Just when I thought he might spook and turn, he broke into a dog-trot past my blind.

"The sixty-five-pound Bear Magnum was drawn and my thirty-yard pin just came up near the point of the shoulder as the bull headed almost straight away. On release, I could see the arrow enter the left hindquarter. My first impression was that it was a 'bad hit,' but the bull almost lost his footing and I saw a large patch of red emerge on his flank."

Two more quick arrows anchored him swiftly, and McCrory had an outstanding trophy. The animal scored 391 and made the Number Two spot in that Pope and Young recording period. McCrory's cabinmate, Paul Brunner, took a bull that same day which made first, scoring 395-6/8.

The third day was my day. The icy mist stung our faces as we pulled ashore four miles downriver from camp that morning. We had a perfect bowhunting set-up. The beach was narrow, and the stand made a cul-de-sac into the tag alders that lined the bank.

We hid and began glassing. After a half-hour, I caught a hint of movement on a granite-topped mountain about three miles away. Silouetted in the rising sun came Tuktu, the Brother to the Wind, with a tremendous rack and a pure white mane that ruffled in the Arctic wind. I will never see a more magnificent sight.

Brunner, who was behind me so he could get everything on film, and Izzy the guide quickly picked him out before he disappeared into the tag elders at the bottom of the mountain, still meandering our way. As the long minutes dragged by, I tried to warm my hands and check my equipment. I was shooting a sixty-three-pound Bear Grizzly II bow with XX75 2117 Jim Dougherty Smokes tipped with Razorback 4 broadheads.

In eighteen minutes (Brunner timed it), the bull broke out of cover on the opposite shore a hundred yards above us. I noted that he was the first bull we had seen out of velvet.

"Old bulls come out of velvet sooner," Isadore informed us.

"Fine bull, hey, Paul?" I asked.

"Fine bulls, you mean. Look to your right," Paul replied.

Ten more huge bulls had broken out of the brush to join their big compadre in the river. They swam toward one of the rifle hunters. We had plenty of time to compare heads. "The biggest is the number three in line, but your bull that's out of velvet ain't no slouch," observed Paul, mocking my Mississippi accent.

When the bulls splashed ashore from the river and

began walking toward us, still five hundred yards away, the biggest bull suddenly collapsed as if the beach had been jerked out from under him. Seconds later, we heard the "ker-boom" of the 7mm. A gun hunter had his Boone and Crockett bull, the biggest in the herd, but at the shot, five other bulls had disappeared in the opposite direction. The other five charged toward us. The big velvetless bull was in this bunch!

I nocked an arrow and backed toward an alder bush thirteen yards from the beach. I could hear the bulls grunting as they ran and the thunder of their enormous hooves on the rocky shore. "Calm down. Pick a spot," I told myself, but it was hard to think with the blood roaring in my ears as the clattering hooves drew closer.

Suddenly the lead bull blasted by me with foam on his lips and huge velvet-covered antlers swaying on his head. From the corner of my eye I could see my quarry approaching, his fifty-inch-wide orange-polished rack towering over the alders.

"Draw now. Pick a spot," I thought, and the arrow was on its deadly way. Brunner's camera whirred behind me as the arrow disappeared behind the bull's last rib, quartering forward.

When our hearts finally calmed to 150 beats a minute, we charged out on the rocky beach and immediately found blood in two parallel paths. The arrow had complete and apparently deadly penetration.

We watched the five big bulls up ahead plunge back into the icy water and start to swim across. When they reached the opposite shore, the four unscathed bulls trotted off, but the old campaigner stood still a moment, then took two steps forward before he fell backward into the shallows. Jubilant is a good word to describe my personal feelings then, as Paul and Izzy and I pounded each other on the back and did an impromptu dance on the beach. Paul told me he'd had almost as much fun getting the whole thing on film as in taking his bull the day before.

The author and Lee Kline bringing home their caribou bulls on the George River

While Izzy and I were dragging my bull back across the river behind our canoe, we paused to watch Charlie Kroll take a fine caribou about 150 yards up the beach from us, which he then towed toward our location. Then Lee Kline ran up.

"Quiet, you guys. Another big bull is trying to cross the river!"

We all dived into the tag alders and watched as the

Veteran bowhunters Lee Kline and Paul Brunner admire the author's caribou.

A shore lunch for the bowhunters—Charlie Kroll, author, Isadore Belvin, Paul Brunner, and Jim McCrory

Author and Charlie Kroll with caribou antlers

bull walked right toward Lee. At the "twang" of the bow, the bull charged straight into the river, reared completely out of the water like a whale, and crashed over backward in a shower of spray. About the same time, Dougherty motored up with another monster rack displayed in the front of his canoe.

The celebration then began anew around a roaring fire with hot tea and sandwiches. Charlie Kroll raised his cup in a toast. "To the greatest bowhunting Caribou Culling Expedition ever, you potlickers!" he said.

"To Charging Gopher, the greatest hunt organizer in history!" we toasted back, as we watched a world-record caribou bull lead his herd across the river.

CINNAMON BEAR

The Fireball Bear

I'm hooked on bear hunting. After a dismal winter, nothing is finer than to be in the Rockies in the spring. The air is dry, crisp, and cool. The wild flowers toss their saucy heads in a kaleidoscope of color. The aspens are heavy with bright new foliage, and the bear (oh, the bear!) are hungrily aroam in their beautiful, thick, winter coats.

The Western Black Bear, *Ursus americanus*, comes in a variety of colors ranging all the way from coal-black through all shades of brown and red to blonde. Taking these handsome critters with either bait or dogs is an exciting, as well as productive, sport.

One fine June day found me happily hunting a friend's bait station high in a quaking aspen tree. The set-up was perfect. Far down the ridge, near a stream below, the bears would lay up in the cool, lush bottom of Uni-

Colorado Bear Country

weep Canyon. Late in the day they would make their way up the mountainside in search of food.

I was on the edge of the Uncompahgre Plateau in western Colorado with a spectacular view of the Book Cliff Mountains to the north. The scene was so lovely that I was only faintly aware of the sickeningly sweet smell of the pile of putrefying hog heads and meat scraps that lay ten yards from my tree stand. As an extra enticement, I had laid a freshly-opened can of sardines on the bait pile.

The already long shadows lengthened down the mountain, and the coyotes' eerie wails began. I shivered in the evening chill and the incomparable wildness of it all. This mountain was my whole world at that moment, and the ancient rhythms of nature burned themselves into the very core of my being. I pity the non-hunter at times like these, but I will grant him his rights as long as he doesn't encroach on mine.

My reverie was soon broken by the sound of a dislodged pebble down on the mountainside. I slowly swiveled my head in that direction, and saw, coming up the mountain, an apparition that I'll never forget. It looked as if a giant orange light bulb was floating up the mountain about a foot off the ground!

As the phantom came closer, it materialized into a beautiful blonde bear with chocolate feet and head.

The bear went for the sardines like a martin to a gourd. The sixty-three-pound Bear Alaskan came up like a feather, and the arrow zipped a deadly path through the bear's vitals.

I have never seen any animal accelerate from standing still to full speed as fast as that bear did. Suddenly, another amazing thing happened. In the rapidly-encroaching darkness, the bear was throwing up a trail of sparks down the mountain!

When it was over, I sat stunned in my tree stand. Was the high altitude causing hallucinations? Had my

Cinnamon Bear

tenuous mind finally snapped? I finally eased down from the tree stand after an anxious and puzzled wait, and tried to find my bear. There was no blood trail, and every boulder on the mountainside was the color of that bear. Darkness stopped my search that night, but the next morning, after a totally sleepless night, I found the bear and the answer to my great riddle.

The steel Black Diamond Delta was sticking down, exposed, out of the bear's chest, and every time he ran over a rock, the steel was indeed striking a trail of sparks!

The beautiful blonde bruin was full mounted and now occupies a prominent place of honor in my game room. All of my mounted bow trophies bring back wonderful hunting memories, but the most unique and bizarre of all is "Old Fireball."

The Fireball Bear

Outfitting for An Extended Hunt for Mountain Game

Back in the days of my youth, my good and great friend, world-class hunter Hugh Nichols, let me tag along on a horseback gun hunt for trophy mule deer in the extremely high Grey's River area near Jackson Hole. The first preparatory thing I did was to order from a war-surplus catalog a mammoth duffle bag that was made in Korea of the type of naugahide that is used to make scabbards for my son's cap pistols. I then proceeded, over a three-month period of time, to stuff immense quantities of every kind of junk imaginable, in duplicate, into it.

Things like giant first aid kits, four boxes of 7mm ammo, three kinds of hunting coats, bales of other clothing, four flashlights of various jumbo sizes, extra food, four pairs of footwear, meat saw, axe, three kinds of knives, and a complete gun cleaning kit, . . . You get the picture! When Hugh arrived to pick me up for the trip to the airport, it took me, Hugh, and the yard man ten minutes to wrestle the bloomin' thing into his

Blazer. Hugh immediately dubbed the behemoth "Big Mama." When we arrived in camp, in Wyoming, he announced to the assemblage after supper that young Ellis had a real treat in store—"Big Mama" would now disgorge a bellydancer and a case of champagne for camp entertainment!

Poor "Big Mama" suffered an ignominious demise at the Denver airport on the way home when both handles pulled out and she ripped from stem to stern, spilling out a largess of equipage that would make a junk dealer drool!

Since then I have modified my equipment list considerably. As I write this, I am preparing for a mixed-bag hunt to the Northwest Territories for Dall sheep and caribou. The following is my basic check list for this hunt, which I modify only slightly for other hunts. For instance, you would not need a large, elaborate backpack for hunting antelope, buffalo, muskox, or the like. A good-quality duffle bag would do just fine with the inclusion of a fanny pack and/or a small day pack.

My basic check list for the sheep hunt:

Plane tickets
Hunting license
Camp Trails vagabond pack
Tubular arrow holder
Canvas and leather "Yukon Guide" day pack
Fanny pack
Eddie Bauer Skyliner full-sized 4-pound down sleeping bag
Sleeping bag stuff bag
Therm-A-rest air mattress
1 308 Garrett Accur-light custom rifle

Left: *Magnificent bugling bull elk in the rut*

Far left, above: *Six Pope and Young caribou trophies for six happy bowhunters: from left, Jim Dougherty, Charlie Kroll, Paul Brunner, author, Lee Kline, and Jim McCrory.*

Far left, below: *Loading the DeHavilland Otter with caribou trophies for the long flight back from the Arctic Circle*

Below: *The author cooking caribou tenderloin at a trapper's cabin in the Yukon territory*

Above: *Goat cliffs of Scapegoat Mountain, Montana*

Left: *Tuktu, Brother to the Wind, in full flight*

Far left, above: *Thundering cataract in Canadian sheep country*

Far left, below: *Chocolate phase black bear and cubs*

Right: *Dall sheep camp in the Mackenzie Mountains of the Northwest Territories*

Below: *A night camp on the ice pack near the North Pole*

Far right: *Yukon pack train bringing out the trophies*

Right: *Hog hunting in the "impassable density of briar and cane" of the Mississippi Delta swamp*

Below: *The Grey Ghosts of Windsor with, from left, Tommy Bourne, author, and Robin Callendar*

2 boxes Federal Premium 165-grain sierra Boat-tails
1 small gun cleaning kit
1 hard bow/gun case custom built by Americase
24 Thunderhead 125 Broadheads
1 Leatherman tool kit
Bear "Grizzly II" sixty-five-pound bow and handmade "Mullen" rope release
18 Easton 2114 xx 75 arrows with 4 inch light helical vanes
1 Quickee Quiver
1 extra pair clear prescription eyeglasses, if needed
1 pair sunglasses
1 small pocketknife
1 medium-sized Gerber Folder knife in belt case
1 small whet stone
1 small tape measure
1 small aluminum waterproof box for survival gear, the cover of which reads "To Billy Ellis, my companion of the autumn trails—Charlie Kroll." This box is always on my person on a hunt (especially in the bush plane), and it fondly reminds me of the old curmudgeon who gave it to me. The lid comes off, and the bottom can be used as a small cooking pot. This box contains:
1 space blanket, 3 heat tabs, 3 match starters, 1 butane lighter, some fishing line, 1 trout lure, and 2 bullion cubes.
1 heavy Cordura bow case with "D Rings" added for saddle attachment
1 pair Danner lightweight Goretex boots (I like Goretex boots because they are light, but they leak just like leather boots, and I take great delight in stopping up all those exquisite high-tech micropores with water-repellant spray before I pack up.)
1 lightweight Eddie Bauer down jacket
1 pair camp shoes
1 lightweight Eddie Bauer two-piece rainsuit

1 camo chamois shirt
1 light cotton camo hunting shirt
2 sets Camo Clan hunting jackets and pants (They're great, but they lack big pouch pockets on the lower pants legs. I order extra cloth and add them. Do not put a patch on the left chest area. My bow string caught the corner of my Pope and Young patch that was sewn there, and I missed a deer. This was known as an Ishi-missee!) I use the Camo Clan WWII dark green camo pattern everywhere when hunting on the ground. For tree stand hunting, I prefer the Trebark pattern.
I also carry:
2 sets duofold two-piece long handles
4 pair "Early Winters" double nylon "blister-proof" socks (to wear under heavy boot socks)
2 pair heavy cotton socks
2 pair heavy wool socks
6 pair boxer shorts
6 pair Penney's extra-long tee shirts, with pockets—in brown, rust, and green
1 Tekna four-cell flashlight
1 small Tekna Micro-Lith flashlight, always in pocket (Wrapped around it is exactly ten yards of trot line tipped with a large snap swivel for laying out target ranges, for pulling a bow up into a tree stand, or for survival use, if necessary.)
2 Bowhunter-type target faces
1 pair Browning leather gloves
1 pair wool mittens
1 Amacker camo face mask
1 Olympus OM-2 35mm camera, Tele-lens, wide-angle lens
15 rolls Ecktachrome 400 ASA film with 36 exposures each
2 garbage bags
1 roll black electrical tape
1 roll packing tape

1 knit stocking cap
1 down cap with ear flaps
1 summer hunting cap
1 winter hunting cap
1 Jones-style waterproof hunting hat
1 pair Bushnell 7 × 26 Custom Compact binoculars
1 Bushnell 10 × 45 "Spacemaster" Spotting scope and matching tripod
1 telescoping light-action six-foot spinning rod
1 light reel with four-pound line and assorted Mepps trout lures
1 small bottle of liquid "Mountain Suds" soap
1 pint poly water bottle
1 brown wash cloth
1 brown medium-sized towel
1 Dopp kit for medicine and toiletries
1 travel alarm clock
1 small can of Snowseal boot waterproofer
1 collapsable drinking cup (indispensible for dipping up water from hard-to-get-to places. Also, if you are on a rock chute and see water trickling through the rocks but can't get to it, you can break off the top and bottom inches of an arrow and use it as a straw. I have seen the time when I would break my bow in two if I could use it to acquire water.)
Tweezers and fingernail clippers
Cigarette lighter
Small mirror
4 Q-Tips
Dental floss
1 comb

I always carry some extra required medicines, such as blood pressure pills, in my pocket pill box and in the survival kit. Have your local doctor help you make up a small batch of emergency medicines when you are packing into remote areas. My kit includes the following:

Lomotil for stomach cramps and diarrhea

Strong antibiotic pills such as Vibramycin and Keflex for upper respiratory or other infections, such as cuts, close encounters of a grizzly kind, etc.

A strong pain killer, such as Darvocet

1 small squeeze bottle of Desenex powder

1 small box of handi-wipes for "spit baths" if water is scarce

Bufferin or Tylenol for the usual aches and pains of a hunt

Neosporin antibiotic ointment

4 inch-square adhesive bandages for blistered heels

8 large Band-Aids

1 large spandex bandage for sprains (yes, I've used it)

1 bottle Cabela's Canadian Deet insect repellant

2 needles and sutures in sterile packs

1 small bottle of Dr. Tichenor's antiseptic (doubles as mouthwash)

Travel toothbrush and toothpaste

Maalox Plus antiacid tablets

Actifed decongestant tablets

Deodorant stick

Dristan Nasal Spray

Orajel toothache gel

Early Winter's Vision AntiFogger for eyeglasses and optics

Ak-Sulf Eye Drops

Visine eye drops

Ducolax laxative pills

Small note pad and pens

Small bar of soap

Cortisporin ear drops

1 small roll surgical tape

small can Shower to Shower body powder

Laundry service in the North Country

Author checking equipment and sharpening broadheads

Gobbler

Your glottal thunder
   echoes of eternity
      in the fog-clad river bottom,

and the first glint of morning sunlight
   shatters the prism of
      iridescent feathers,

while nuances of Nineveh
   are printed in cuneiform
      with the passage
         of your track.

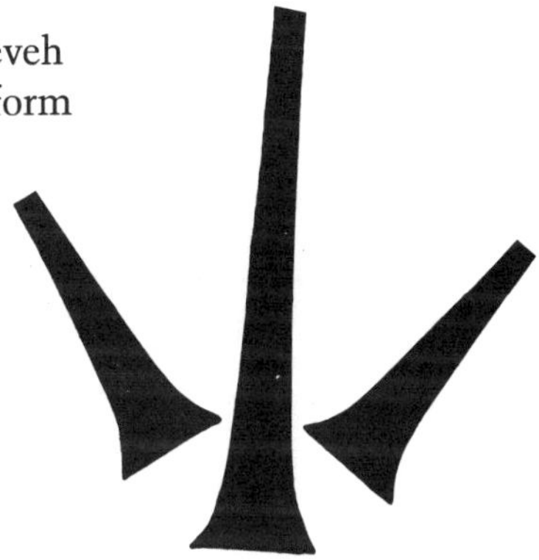

The scenic road General Grant took as it looks today

WHITETAIL DEER

The Grey Ghosts of Windsor

From high atop my tree stand, I could look down on the flood plain of the mighty Mississippi River and the narrow winding road that once bore the traffic of the largest marine invasion force ever assembled prior to Normandy. My mind's eye went back to the Civil War, and I could see the seemingly endless double columns of blue-coated soldiers and the skirmishers crawling like ants over the flanks and front.

General Ulysses S. Grant sat stoically in the saddle. His complicated order of battle and the fear of early detection of his landing weighed heavily upon him. Suddenly, like an opulent dream of days gone by, an exquisite Greek Revival mansion belonging to a local planter-aristocrat named Smith Daniel loomed ahead of the dusty, sweating column. A major on the point rode back to Grant.

"Do we give 'er the torch, General?" inquired the officer.

"Spare Windsor," Grant grunted through teeth clenched around his omnipresent cigar. "It belongs to former friends of ours from Illinois, and besides, the smoke might alert the Confederates at Port Gibson."

Thus, by a quirk of fate, possibly the finest Southern Planter's home of its type was spared the ravages of war. After the cessation of hostilities, it again heard the careless laughter, the clink of champagne glasses, and the lilt of the parlor orchestra, as the Southern Belles pirouetted in their hoop-skirted organdy and crinoline dresses. It was at such a soiree in 1891 that a carelessly-tossed cigarette caused the fire that totally destroyed her. Today, the ghostly columns of Windsor still stand amongst some of the finest whitetail deer habitat in North America. Here still roam the true "Grey Ghosts of Windsor."

A leading whitetail expert named Robin Callendar is outfitting for these grey ghosts at his Cedar Ridge Hunting Preserve, which encompassed 6,500 acres of prime habitat for deer, wild turkey, and wild Russian boar. I was trying out his weekend bowhunters' special, which turned out to be a fantastic hunt.

My first stand was an Amacker Deer Thief Deluxe tree-climbing stand that overlooked a heavily-laden honey locust grove. A fine Oklahoma bowhunter named Jim Harvey had spotted a large buck feeding there the afternoon before. A full hour before dark, I heard a towboat foghorn weave its mournful melody across the Mighty Mississippi. As the sun started to set, I heard a barely perceptible crunch of leaves and looked up to see two does tipping in to the locust tree. I strained my eyes to see a buck.

By now the does were chomping hungrily on the sweet fermented bean pods. The largest threw her head up; she had caught a slight whiff of my scent on my entrance trail. She and her companion started that old familiar "straight-leg-shuffle" that deer do when slightly alarmed. I had a decision to make. Should I wait for the buck? "Not on a short hunt," I thought, and my bow came up.

I took what I thought was good aim at the biggest doe at twenty-eight yards, released, and watched the arrow zip right under the deer and plow into the bean pods which littered the ground. The old doe came unglued in the blink of an eye. I still remember her rocketing straight up into the air with a bean pod hanging from the corner of her mouth.

It soon grew dark, and as I was retrieving my Emerson XX75 arrow tipped with a Thunderhead 125, Robin and Tulsa Jim pulled up in Robin's pickup. "From the woebegone look on your face, Billy, you missed," opined my outfitter. "Look in the back!" There lay Jim's first deer, and he was ecstatic.

However, at Cedar Ridge, the emphasis is on hunting, not partying, so we kept the pre-supper toasts to a minimum when we returned to the lodge. As a heavenly aroma wafted from the kitchen, my thoughts turned back to camp cooks I had known.

The worst was an elk-camp cook that our outfitter was forced to drag in drunken disarray out of a flophouse in Missoula, Montana. His gastronomic attempts had ranged from bland to bilious, and what personality that managed to seep out of the booze-ravaged brain had been reminiscent of a Grizzly with a toothache. To be charitable, let's just say that he was not a graduate of the Cordon Bleu in Paris. Not so with Robin's Head

of Culinary Delights, Jack Partridge. His ebullient good humor boils over into his cooking, which has become legendary. His venison spaghetti that first night was fit for a fair maid of Windsor.

After supper, we all made plans for the next day. The two Tulsa bowmen liked their previous stands and wanted to return to them in the morning. "How would you like to try for the 'Dawn Express'?" Robin asked me.

"Great! What's the deal?" I replied.

"There is a huge buck that leaves a milo field before daylight, tips way back into the woods, and lays low before shooting light. You may, just may, catch him coming through late enough to get a shot. All he has to do is tarry with a doe just one morning and we'll hang him on the meat pole!" quoth Robin.

The night flew by, and a full hour before daylight, Jack's son, Keith Partridge, and I tipped blindly through the woods to my stand. We were playing it safe and not using a flashlight. A distant group of hoot owls went through their laughing hyena routine. The cacophony of sound motivated several jake gobblers to try out their adolescent vocal chords. It was a marvelous cackle contest.

Then came a hint of pink in the eastern sky. I could see my hands, but I couldn't see the ground. The awful seconds ticked by . . . "Hold back, hold back, Grey Ghost," I whispered, in what I knew in my heart was a litany of dispair. Forms vaguely materialized: the trunks of trees, a bush or two.

"Chweek, chweek, chweek!" Hoofsteps were coming up the hill right toward me. "Not yet!" I thought, but oh, yes, as sure as death and bank examinations, he was coming on in—way too soon! My eyes stood out of their sockets. "I've got to see him!" I thought.

"Wheew! Wheew!" He blew right at me just to let me know he knew that I was in the tree. Then the final act of defiance: instead of racing away, he started coming right at me! He knew I was there, and he also knew I couldn't see to shoot. "Chweek, chweek!"

A slight aura glowed around him. His massive horns took on abstract proportions in the surreal pre-dawn madness that was somehow mixed with the pulsing of the blood in my eyes and temples. He swaggered in macho majesty right by my tree as invisible as a Ninja. Then he ghosted up the hill and out of my life forever.

The great whitetail authority Gene Wenzel says he is certain that old bucks can discern human brain waves. This incident further bears that out!

The rest of the morning was anti-climatic, even though I saw twenty-nine wild turkey hens and jakes. After a mid-day rest, I was raring to get back into the woods as the two fine Tulsa bowhunters, the Harvey brothers, were pulling out for home. They each reported a wonderful hunt. I opted to try Jim's stand, since he had taken a doe and seen nine more deer and a herd of wild hogs which contained two huge boars.

We again drove by the ruins of Windsor and wound deeper into the lush hardwood river bottoms. We stopped Robin's pickup and hiked a mile back into the heavy timber to a beautiful meandering creek with high banks. A deeply etched deer trail came out of the woods to the right of my tree stand, which stood high in a large willow tree. The trail then crossed the creek and bore up the steep bank to my right and then on out into an eighty-acre soybean field which the deer had ravaged.

The weather was wonderful, with low humidity and a hint of fall in the air. I re-hashed the morning's adventure and admired several red-tailed hawks and kingfishers as they made their living, catching rodents and fish in this verdant river bottom. Then a flicker of brown caught my eye.

Seconds ticked by. Another flicker of movement up the trail, and here they came! A nice herd of deer with several big yearlings and three nice, fat does. My decision was quick. I would attempt to tag the old lead doe.

On they tipped, down the far bank, then across the creek. Now the old big doe swung around to my right. My mental computer went into high: "How far? How far?" The bow was up. Thirty, thirty-five yards, thirty-six.

"Whap!" The deer hit the sand, then was back up as the whole herd bolted back across the creek. The lead deer was almost to the top of the high bank when she suddenly reared up, fell over backward, and slid back down to the water's edge. "Number twenty," I thought as that feeling of exhilaration that I had felt nineteen other times came flooding over me.

It had been a wonderful day, and right then and there I thanked the Good Lord for the whitetail deer. I also reflected on my failure to take the giant buck that morning, and I remembered a classic English poem that had pertinence to my hunt. This poem had been especially popular when Windsor mansion had flourished. In *Ode to a Grecian Urn*, John Keats describes the flutist's eternal quest for the nubile maidens who dance forever out of reach. A perfect analogy for my elusive dream of a trophy Grey Ghost of Windsor:

. . . What leaf-fringed legend haunts about thy shape
What mad pursuit? What struggle to escape? . . .
. . . Heard melodies are sweet, but those unheard
Are sweeter; therefore, ye soft pipes, play on. . . .

Author in front of the ruins of Windsor

To my hunting buddy, Dr. Andy Reese,
as unique as he was lovable.
Lord, I wish he had worn a safety belt
on his last bowhunt.

Requiem for a Hunter

Slowly the cortege winds
  through fallow fields
    now frozen in oblivion.

As the still stranger whose legacy
  is now the mallards' chuckle
    the children's laughter, and the April rain.

With stifling tension, drones the pastoral tribute
  to the lovable leprechaun,
    who daily moved in higher grace
      than these contrived obsequies.

In choked silence, the banal platitudes
  blaspheme down His cross and mine;
    gnarling the dogwoods.

And I remember not his twisted spine,
    but his eye's brave glint;
our last gobbler strutting through the yellow-tops,
  the woody hen nesting by his back door,
and old "Smut," his lab, looking everywhere for him
    this awful morning.

I shall sow my last salt tear
in the tattered apron of old Liza,
her ancient face now turned to stone.

And as swiftly gone as the migrating mallard,
the old dog, and the April rain,
I return no more.

JAVELINA

Javelina and Woolly Bullys

I had been daydreaming about bowhunting for a different species of North American big game when the phone rang. "How would you like to meet me in Texas and hunt some javelina?" boomed the indomitable outdoor writer, photographer, and guide, Judd Cooney, of Pagosa Springs, Colorado.

"How would you like to have Vanna White for a traveling photography assistant?" I retorted.

"I'm not kidding, Ellis. I've got some friends at McAllen, Texas, who have invited me and a companion to bowhunt and photograph a selection of critters. Can you go?" asked Cooney.

"When do we leave?" I blurted excitedly.

One week later, in the shank of October, we started our memorable hunt.

"Get ready!" exclaimed Judd as he put the clear plastic critter call to his lips. I was standing in front of him at fifteen yards, waist deep in prickly-pear cactus and

thorn bush, my bow at half-draw. The shrieks and moans that then emanated from that caller would have made the Marquis de Sade chuckle with pleasure. Hideous sounds of unspeakable torture reverberated through the Texas brush country.

"Ka-whump!" An iron-gray fireball raced right for my legs, teeth popping and little red eyes aflame! I jumped straight up in the air and did a Gabby Hays buck dance at the same time.

"Squeeunk!" Another javelina darted in with malice aforethought.

"Shoot! Shoot!" roared Judd. At that point, my only thought was to keep from being permanantly disabled as still another javelina darted in, teeth chattering, presenting only a head shot. I came to full draw, hoping he'd turn broadside, but the critters whirled away and disappeared. I had to let my bow down.

"Why didn't you shoot?" boomed a disconcerted Cooney.

"I . . . I . . . I . . . No comment!" I muttered.

"Welcome to javelina hunting!" quoth my grinning partner.

Javelina are a lot like FDIC bank examiners. They usually run in packs, they have sharp teeth which can inflict severe retribution if provoked, and they are basically argumentative in nature. Adult javelina average 35 pounds and are swift, agile, and muscular, making them challenging animals to hunt with a bow. Their eyesight, while not on a par with antelope or sheep, is adequate, and their senses of hearing and smell are excellent. They are also very tenacious for life, and a well-placed heart-lung shot is a necessity since the brush country they inhabit is virtually impenetrable. Trailing a wounded animal in this habitat could possibly become a study in futility, due to the fact that all of the vegetation either claws, sticks, stings, or all of the above.

Author with javelina trophy and Judd Cooney

After the "attack" was over, I experienced a searing pain in my left chest. "This is the 'Big One' that bankers and air-traffic controllers are noted for," I feared. I sat down, unbuttoned my shirt, and there in the left pectoral (a part of the anatomy made famous by Dolly Parton) was a prickly-pear spine jammed an inch into my chest. I could not pull it out and had to have my guide to assist. I wished I had brought some local anesthetic, or at least some tequila, for the operation.

Judd and I were hunting the Guajolota ranch near McAllen, Texas. Man has his biblical allotted time on earth, and so had we on this ranch. Fate next found us on the La Media Ranch nearby, and there we found a veritable paradise on earth.

The hunting operation was managed by the handsome and genial Robert Rogers, whose books, *Great Whitetails of North America, Volumes I and II,* are classics in their genre. His operation was first class, from his fabulous hunting lodge laid out around a large swimming pool to his staff consisting of expert guides Danny Estes and Glen Ringstaff. The delicious food services were maintained by Danny's wife Mary Sue, and the whole shoot-and-shebang received the tender loving care of Robert's wife Cindie.

"Javelina? Sho! We'll get you as many as you want!" exclaimed Danny.

"How about *one*?" I retorted.

"Nooooo problem."

I am always skeptical of the colloquialism "no problem," a by-word of the Taltan Indians of the Cassiar Mountains of Northern British Columbia. Everytime one of them told me "Nooooo problem," I usually had problems in bucketfuls, like hanging by my fingernails on a granite face over a 2,000-foot drop.

We soon loaded up in one of the camp pickups and started off on our javelina hunt. Two of the assistant guides were in the back of the pickup and the rest of us were up front. We had not gone over a mile down a sendero (a road-size opening through the thick Texas brush) when "bam, bam" went a fist on top of the pickup and someone cried, "Javelina! Javelina! Javelina!" The truck screeched to a halt.

"Over there!" rasped Danny. I grabbed my bow and gingerly sidled my way into the thorn bushes and prickly-pear cactus, remembering the thorny episode of the previous day. I let my eyes do most of the stalking. Javelina have almost perfect camoflauge in the South Texas Brush Country.

"That prickly-pear up the hill seems awfully black," I thought. Through my Bushnell Custom Compacts the object still looked strange. Then it moved almost imperceptibly. "Javelina!" my brain flashed.

My Bear Grizzly II came up, and I eased to my right to ascertain which part of the pig I was looking at. I made out his heart-lung zone, the sight settled in at twenty yards and "thwack!" it was a solid hit. Sounding like a runt rhino, the penetrated porker instantly disappeared through the fierce thorn brush.

"Unghhh! Thump!" Another javelina jumped out, and almost ran between my legs. I fumbled to retrieve another arrow but in a flash he whirled and was gone, too. "This javelina hunting can be high excitement!" I thought.

There is an ancient joke that I heard in grammer school, about an introverted little boy who had a small but extremely ferocious critter which he carried around in a little cage tucked under his arm. This creature had various names, depending on who was telling the joke, but I heard it as "Woolly Bully." Now ole "Woolly Bully" would attack anything quicker than General A. P. Hill would tear into General Burnside's flank (and that, my friends, is fast and furious!)

The joke goes that the little boy from time to time would shout, "Woolly Bully! That dog!" and pop the little cage door open, and instantaneously, ole "Woolly Bully" would reduce the huge mutt into Hamburger Helper. Various other animals were also subjected to nameless indignities before the joke's punch line. At the end, the town bully comes up to the shy little boy, hits him in the mouth, and asks the pitiful fellow, "What's in the cage?"

"A Woolly Bully," sniffles the hapless hero.

"Woolly Bully, my ass!" booms the bully, . . . and the little boy pops the cage door open!

In about thirty seconds, I was about to witness two woolly bullies collide. La Media had a fabulous sheep dog that is also a champion blood trailer and attack

Razor-sharp tusk of a javelina

dog. When my friends in the pickup heard the arrow hit and saw the javelina race away, they unsnapped the dog's leash and undoubtedly ordered "Woolly Bully! That javelina!" Like Admiral Yamamoto at Midway, little did I know that *three* forces were converging toward one point, with very interesting consequences.

"Baaoouu! Baaoouu! Snap, unghh! eweeuunh!" A terrible scuffle had erupted in a little opening in the brush. I un-nocked my arrow and hastened gingerly toward the conflict.

The second I broke out into the opening, the dog grabbed the javelina by the nose. Old *Tayassu tajacu* slung the dog away and looked for something else to charge. That something else was me! With teeth popping and eyes blazing, the real woolly bully forced me to jump backward—right square into another prickly-pear!

As the javelina bit at my heels, the dog attacked the mini-monster's flanks, and the valiant little creature turned away from me to meet his new threat. This gave me time to re-nock an arrow, and the Thunderhead 125 broadhead walloped him hard. Yet he grabbed the dog by an ear and flipped over backward into a brier-filled depression.

After some hideous squalls and anxious moments, the brave but battered dog crawled out of the hole, but the javelina did not. He will achieve porcine immortality, however, in the form of a full mount by museum-quality taxidermist Tommy Ramage. He was not only brave, he was a very large boar, and had afforded me a wonderfully exciting hunt.

As my guide pulled the barbed cactus thorns from my posterior, I had an occasional moment of anguish and decided that javelina are wonderful trophies, but before you get too close, remember the "Woolly Bully!"

ANTELOPE

Jousting with Windmill Pronghorns

After three days of frustrated waiting and tension, the culmination of months of planning, a handsome pronghorn buck was finally coming in to the waterhole. The does and yearlings seemed to sense no danger whatsoever, but the buck was suspicious. Viewed through my Bushnell 7 × 26 Custom Compacts, he looked larger than life. Like Clint Eastwood in a "Spaghetti Western," he was coming in with drama and purpose, taking short, deliberate steps. The shimmering heat waves mantled him in a surreal aura.

One hundred yards and closing the gap! I hung my binoculars aside and eased the Bear Grizzly II into position. The wind was gusting now to thirty knots, but it was blowing in my favor. The six does cautiously eased up to the waterhole and began to drink. The big buck hung back at sixty yards and nervously pranced from side to side. The does finally finished drinking and began to move off slowly. The buck began to move in. And buck fever began to move in also, extending its tendrils over my frame. My blood pressure was approaching critical mass.

At twenty-eight yards, the buck stopped and looked back at the does. Would he turn away and follow them or come forward to drink? It was now or never. I made a smooth, fast draw, trying to remember the basics: pick a spot, keep back tension, follow through, and the arrow was on its way. The release felt fine, but the arrow began fish-tailing in the strong wind. I watched helplessly as it struck a clump of sage at the buck's feet. The animal seemed to levitate and perform a one-eighty simultaneously. Then he shifted into overdrive as only a pronghorn can.

At that moment, I completely changed my attitude concerning bowhunting antelope. A big buck with his smart brown, white, and black pelage, topped with rakish jet-black horns, is definitely a worthy bow trophy. Granted, pursuit is not as exciting or as earthshaking as calling a huge lustful elk or moose into your lap, but nevertheless, it is a great thrill to observe the prairie speedsters in their own bailiwick and hope for an occasional buck to approach close enough for a shot.

Antelope generally inhabit the mile-high arid vastness of the great western plains. Aside from a temporary setback in North Dakota, where an extremely severe winter drastically reduced their herds, these animals thrive throughout the Plains States. In 1924, after years of exploitation by market hunting, there were

The big buck that got away

only 26,700 pronghorns in the entire country. But thanks to intelligent game management, with carefully regulated and licensed hunting as a control factor, the population is presently estimated at some 406,000-plus animals. Wyoming is first in population density with about 168,000. Controlled sport hunting continues as the most effective means known to keep the herds within the carrying capacity of the ranges.

From my personal observation, the pronghorn does not compete with sheep and cattle for food. The antelope seem to prefer sage and other browse plants, while livestock prefer grasses. It is also noteworthy that antelope have a high immunity to common livestock diseases, which is fortunate, since they all use the same mineral licks and water sources.

Antelope are unusual and eccentric animals and are fun to watch. I once witnessed a young buck chase a large coyote for several hundred yards. I had always thought it was vice versa. On another occasion, I saw a medium-sized buck do battle with a small buck and then run him out of the herd. The victor then made a triumphant lap around the does, with all the arrogance and aplomb of a matador who had just vanquished a Muria bull and been awarded both ears and the tail.

Antelope hunting is also relatively inexpensive, compared to other big-game bowhunts. My hunt for one week included a twenty-five-dollar trespass fee, two dollars a night for a mobile home bunkhouse, a ten-dollar archery license, one hundred dollars for an antelope tag, and a five-dollar application fee.

The huge ranch on which we were hunting lay in Area 28 north of Douglas, Wyoming, and contained a uranium mine and numerous producing oil wells. Neither of these seemed to bother the antelope. This bares out the fact that wildlife can not only survive but can flourish in areas where our natural resources are being harvested, provided that intelligent drilling and mining practices are followed and sufficient suitable habitat is left undisturbed.

Pronghorns have become accustomed to the creaking and motion of the windmills, which some hunters use as "tree" stands. This is definitely in favor of the bowman. I used no camoflauge make-up or head net as I would have at ground level, for these animals seldom look up. I also used chewing tobacco while on the stand, and the antelope did not seem to notice. I assume they are used to this as a result of ranchers working around the windmills.

I was lucky enough to have been invited to tag along on this hunt with six fine other bowhunters from above the Mason-Dixon line. They had been successful on previous hunts, having taken several Pope and Young-class antelope. It took three days, with the aid of sign language, for them to partially understand my Mississippi accent!

After the first day's scouting, the rancher had lamented the fact that uncommon rainstorms the previous week had decreased our chances considerably; the pronghorns could now get water at any of the numerous puddles left by the rain, instead of having to come to the windmill ponds. His worries had been well-founded, and we experienced slow hunting all week. I was seldom bored, however, as I had been in almost constant visual contact with pronghorns, hawks, ducks, mule deer, eagles, coyotes, and other prairie denizens.

The author in his windmill stand

Hunting from windmills requires some Yankee Ingenuity, to say the least. The platforms atop the windmills are either cramped or non-existant, so we improvised by wedging long boards over and under the metal framework of the tower, attaching a platform of plywood or smaller boards to it. Once the stand was prepared, it was helpful to pace off shooting distances to various points on the waterhole, to salt blocks, etc.

Moonlight over antelope country

On the second day of the hunt, our party, which included Bill Bean, Dr. Dan Davis, Mark Smith, Bob Miller, and Bob Fillbrant, was delighted when a smaller group of veteran bowhunters from Washington state, Steve and Donna Gorr and Jack Williams, joined us. We celebrated that evening with a delicious antelope barbeque.

The days passed and the hunt was swiftly drawing to a close. Nearly everyone had scored, with Steve Gorr taking a record-class buck on the third day. Gorr is one of those bowhunters with the innate ability to scout an area, weigh all the factors, then consistently choose the right spot for an ambush. The final day, I chose to sit on the windmill where he had taken his big pronghorn. I was glassing a large herd containing a few good bucks when intuition warned me to turn around.

I did so and saw an approaching group of twelve animals, led by an old doe with quite well-developed horns. After their usual hesitation, they came in to the water, some thirty yards from me. When the lead doe's head was down, I made a slow draw, got off a smooth release, and watched the 2117 arrow tipped with a Razorback 4 take the animal at the junture of neck and shoulder, burying itself to the feathers. The pronghorn took off at full speed, but on reaching the crest of a small hill some eighty-five yards away, she cartwheeled tail over head, and never moved another muscle. I was thankful for the fast, humane kill and for taking an animal on the last day of the hunt.

As I was field dressing my antelope, I spied a large herd led by a tremendous buck skylined against a spectacular prairie sunset. I vowed, "Come by here for a drink next year, old buddy, and I'll handle the tab. My shooting tab, that is!"

* * *

The author and his fine Pope and Young antelope

True to my promise, I returned the next bow season to the Smith sheep ranch for an antelope buck. Accompanying me were my two long-time bowhunting buddies, Charlie Kroll and Jim McCrory.

During the first two days of the hunt, all three of us scored on excellent Pope and Young record-class bucks. While there, we were entertained at an antelope barbeque by veteran bowhunters George Moerlein, Scott Showalter, Jack Williams, and Pope and Young Club founder Glen St. Charles. They were ensconced in Showalter's tepee on the Wyoming prairie.

That night, we sat around the inner edge of the tepee as the rhythms of the open fire cast eerily-dancing Indian-like shadows on the tent walls. After supper we listened to Glen St. Charles narrate his and Fred Bear's bowhunting tales from days long ago in the Little Delta region of Alaska, and of their hunts for the Great Brown Bear.

Suddenly a high tremulous wail seemed to float down upon the tepee. George Moerlein was standing outside, high on a promontory in the moonlight, playing "Loch Lomond" on his bagpipes. No sound before or since has ever sounded sweeter!

BISON

Trophy Buffalo in the Snow

The old buffalo bull seemed to levitate, then, with pounding hooves, he thundered straight at me in the knee-deep snow! My guide, Les Severson, yelled a warning and grabbed his .44 magnum before he dove behind a tree. At that point, I didn't have a particular escape plan. I couldn't decide whether to breast the deep snow or burrow down under it. Mercifully, the ancient campaigner slowed his charge and finally stood pawing the snow, regarding us (a-la Ruark) as if we owed him money.

The American Buffalo is a unique animal, surrounded by history, sorrow, and mystique. The entire culture of the Plains Indian is inexorably meshed with this magnificent animal, and I am proud to have taken one with semi-traditional archery equipment, under fair-chase conditions.

To the Indian, Pte, the buffalo, was the personification of Wakan Tanka, The Great Spirit. A major part of the Indian's round of life was entwined with the ebb and flow of the great buffalo herds. One early railroad surveyor noted, "From an observation point with our field glasses, we judged the whole space, say five miles by twelve miles, was a seemingly solid mass of buffaloes. . . . they were running as rapidly as a horse can go at a keen gallop; about twelve miles an hour."

Aside from the spiritual manifestation, the buffalo was a major food source for the Indian, who also used virtually every other part of the animal in his daily life. The hide was used for shelter and clothing as well as for shields, drums, rattles, and forty other ceremonial and utilitarian objects. The hair was used for pillow stuffing, saddle pads, ropes, and medicine balls. The tail was used for medicine switches; the horn for cups, spoons, and headdress ornaments; the hooves for glue; the skulls for religious totems; the brains for hide tanning; the sinew for bowstrings; the bladder for medicine bags; the bones for knives, arrow points, shovels, scrapers, awls, and needles. The stomach was used as a cooking vessel and for storing water. Even the buffalo chips were used, for fuel and ceremonial smoking—a custom I'm glad the Anglo-Saxon never adopted!

I have had a great love and affinity for the Plains Indians for most of my life. Among the favorite relics in my collection are a pair of beaded buffalo hide moccasins owned and worn by Chief Short Bull of the Brule Sioux, the great Sioux holy man Black Elk's buffalo headdress, a necklace of artifacts picked up at the Little Big Horn battlefield by Chief High Eagle, and some quill work objects done by my friend Tony Horse Road, the great contemporary Sioux Indian artist. My favorite painting in my art collection is of the Plains Indians on a Buffalo hunt, by Michael Schreck. It captures all of the excitement and drama recorded in 1832 by George Catlin in *Among the Hidatsu*. The painting depicts the hunters galloping their horses around the herd and driving their whizzing arrows or long lances into the hearts of the animals:

"In many instances, the buffaloes, enraged at the painful weapons in their sides, erected their shaggy manes over their bloodshot eyes and plunged forward at the sides of their assailants' horses, sometimes goring them to death at a lunge and putting the dismounted riders to flight for their lives. At times the dense crowd was opened and the blinded horsemen, too intent on their prey amidst a cloud of dust, were hemmed and wedged in amongst the crowding beasts. They were obliged to leap to safety over the animals' backs, leaving their horses to the fate that might await them in this wild and desperate war."

Many were the bulls that turned upon their assailants, meeting them with desperate resistance, and many were the warriors who were dismounted, saving themselves by the superior muscles of their legs. Some who were closely pursued by the bulls suddenly wheeled, and snatching hold of a buffalo robe from around their waist, threw it over the horns and eyes of the beast.

This allowed them to dart in by the animal's side and drive an arrow or lance into its heart.

After the hunt they sang this song:

". . . Man, he has come in with happiness.

Buffalo, them I have taken. . . ."

General Sherman, who also made life rather unpleasant around the South some years back, once said, "A good Indian is a dead Indian!" His unfortunate philosophy also extended to the Indian's *raison d'etre,* the buffalo, and they were slaughtered by the millions. Excellent game management reversed the population decline, and the great shaggy beast is now thriving in certain areas of North America. The largest land animal on the continent, an average full-grown male weighs in at one ton of brute strength and is more than ten feet long, standing six feet at the hump.

To bowhunt one of these tremendous creatures had been one of my ambitions for many years. There is a catch, however. The only places eligible for a Pope and Young animal are the Henry Mountains of Utah and in Alaska, for residents only. After trying unsuccessfully for a Utah permit for several years, I had chosen a fair-chase hunt for a Safari Club-record animal with noted outfitter Alan Baier of Collbran, Colorado. He was highly recommended by two gun-hunting friends of mine, world-class hunter Hugh Nichols and Weatherby award-winner Butch White.

The Baier Ranch was as beautiful as it was rugged. Nestled in the Rocky Mountains, it was between eight

Buffalo country

and nine thousand feet in altitude. Couple this with five-foot snow drifts in February, and a hunter could have about as tough a fair-chase hunt as he would care to have. Our plan for the hunt was to ride the high ridges on snowmobiles and glass the ravines and creek bottoms for the big bulls.

Baier's guides and equipment were excellent, and I was paired with Les Severson, who was canny, lean, and whip-leather tough. The cold and deep snow made the hunting difficult, and the stark scenery was desolate but beautiful. We rode and glassed for miles, and on several occasions I completely buried my machine in the deep snow drifts. Finally, about noon, Severson told me to wait on top of a wind-swept ridge while he made a circuit through a deep creek bottom. After about ten minutes, I heard the full-bore scream of his snowmobile racing toward me. As he roared into view, Severson was waving his hat and I knew that he had located something.

"Two big bulls on the other side of the ridge!" he yelled. We quickly dismounted and crawled to the brow of the crest. Far below, two magnificent old bulls plodded through the snow. As I studied them through my Bushnell Custom Compacts, visions of the early Indian hunters crowded my mind: the Phantom Host of the Sioux Buffalo Honoring Society mounted on their galloping paint ponies, pressing ever closer to the thundering bulls to place an obsidian-tipped arrow through their mighty ribs.

The buffalo were moving along at a steady pace, so

we had to formulate an immediate plan of attack. We decided to drive around the mountain, park the snowmobiles, and climb back up onto a high notch that we hoped the bulls would walk through for a perfect bow set-up. About twenty minutes later, we started our climb. It was extremely difficult because the snow would hold our weight for a second, then we would break through the crust, scraping our shins in the process.

We had been out of visual contact with the bulls for some time, and now we stalked with belabored breath in the high altitude. "I see his hump!" Severson exclaimed breathlessly. I slowly eased up behind my guide and there below us, coming up the steep snowy draw, was a sight to remember. Two giant bulls in glorious winter pelage, their great shaggy heads swinging from side to side, with thick skull ruffs and long flowing beards.

"Take the one on the right!" whispered Severson, when the bulls plodded into bow range. My Bighorn Custom recurve came up and the Kustom King cedar arrow, tipped with a Black Diamond Eskimo, sang in the thin Colorado air. The arrow sank up to the feathers through the liver, much to my chagrin, but the big bull buckled at the knees, and I knew I had a lethal hit.

We waited for a while and pushed him for a short distance until I could get close enough for a *coup de gras* arrow. When this arrow hit, the incident occured that began my story: he charged!

What a magnificent sight it was—the giant head

down, a loud trumpet from those mighty lungs, tail held high, with snow exploding under his thundering hooves. Then he crashed down into the snow. I had my Safari Club silver medal trophy!

If I had been a Plains Indian, or at least all by myself at that instant, I would probably have raised the Sioux buffalo chant:

Strike ye our land
With curved horns!
Now with cries
Bending our bodies,
Breathe fire upon us;
Now with feet
Trampling the earth,
Let your hoofs
Thunder over us!
The buffalo I've taken
And I lift up my voice;
Strike ye our land
With curved horns!

The author and his trophy Buffalo in the snow

Cat country in Idaho

COUGAR
Triple Trophy Cat

The old cougar's rheumy eyes strained to catch even a fleeting glimpse of movement in the driving snow. Old age had finally caught up with her; her ribs showed more plainly with each passing day. She had whelped her last cubs many years ago, and in these final days, she was barely subsisting on small game. Her tattered ears perked up. Hounds! And they were hot on her trail!

A mountain lion hunt, in my opinion, is a glorified 'coon hunt. The differences include the magnificent quarry, the dizzying heights, and the precipitous terrain. My hunt started as they all do: miles and miles of monotonous driving in a four-wheel-drive pickup with the dogs growling and complaining in the zero-degree weather and the dog man trying to keep his and my spirits up by promising a huge set of tracks around each bend in the road. The elusive creatures can be successfully hunted only by finding their tracks in the snow and casting a pack of dogs on the trail. When the lion is treed, the hunter then attempts to move in close enough to make a clean kill.

My guide, Ken Smith, sat amid his own thoughts. The snow had been falling, but only in the high country. A quarter of the terrain was covered, which gave a small chance of striking a lion's track. A "big norther" was building over the White Cloud Mountains near Challis, Idaho, where we were heading. As we wound further up into the high country, the snow thickened. A huge silvery male coyote, as big as a timberwolf, trotted across a snow field.

"Tracks!" Ken suddenly shouted, hitting the brakes. We excitedly jumped out of the truck. Gerald Hansen, the dog handler, pulled out his steel tape and measured the stride.

"Big male lion," he called. The problem was that the tracks were old. They had probably been made the night before. After stomping around a while, Smith and Hansen decided not to cast the hounds. We could possibly lose them on a cold trail, and that would ruin the day.

Disappointed, we kept going on up into the ruggedly beautiful mountains on the east fork of the Salmon River. "Tracks again!" Again the measuring and evaluating.

"Probably came across here early this morning, judging from the snow deposits in the punch holes," Hansen said. The lion puts each foot almost straight down into the snow and picks it up the same way, leaving almost perfectly round, large punched holes, with paw-prints in the bottom.

It was about two in the afternoon, and the go/no-go time was at hand. Smith and Hansen decided the tracks were too old to cast on.

"We'll pull on up to that creek, turn around, and head back," Smith said. A raging brook cut across the road, and the water was almost too deep for a four-wheel-drive vehicle to cross. On the other side the road wound invitingly up the mountain.

"I believe I'll wade across that creek and jog a way up the road," I said. "I want to try out my lowlander's lungs." I jogged about a quarter-mile, enjoying the blue luminous beauty of the mountain with its beautiful undefiled road. Suddenly, up ahead was a sight to warm the heart of the most jaded hunter: a red-hot set of cat tracks!

I ran back as fast as I could, and the team swung into action. Ken Smith splashed across the ford in the truck. After examining the tracks, he concluded that they were made by either a large female or a medium-sized male. We weighed the odds of cutting another hot track on this hunt, and I nodded. "Let's go!"

The three bluetick hounds hit the ground running and mouthing. Everybody somehow went off on a separate course, following the music of the hounds. This song ended abruptly about a half-hour later, when a full-scale blizzard hit the mountain. I was by then exhausted, winded, and alone. My shouts were quickly drowned by the whining of the winter wind, and I decided to back under a ponderosa pine and wait.

About an hour later, Smith appeared as an apparition in the whiteout. "The cat is treed! It's a big old female that Gerald and Gary Power tagged last year. The problem is, the cat's about three miles away, through rough terrain. It's four o'clock and shooting light is fading fast. Do you want to try it?"

"You bet!" I shouted, plunging into the snow, and also into the toughest ordeal I have ever faced in my hunting career.

The cat had wisely chosen the roughest, most precipitous route imaginable. Many times I fell, cursing, barking my shins and knees on the sharp rocks. I was glad that I had my arrows in a covered quiver, and that I had protected the bowstring from sharp rocks by putting plastic tape over it. My bow and I were really taking a beating as we backtracked in the thick snow. I fell into many snow banks, each time too exhausted to continue. The shadows were deepening on the mountain, however, reminding me that I had to get up and go on.

Suddenly, above the blizzard's whine, I heard the tremulous wail of the bluetick hounds, barking treed. My spirits soared, and I was filled with renewed purpose. After another agonizing thirty minutes I reached the tree. The last two hundred yards, littered with fanny pack, jacket, gloves, and canteen, looked like the roads behind the route marches of Stonewall Jackson's foot calvery.

In the dying sunlight, I saw the quarry, a beautiful old mistress of the high and lonely places. The golden, glowing eyes seemed to pierce into my soul as I questioned what impulse had driven me to travel 2,000 miles to this gnarled tree on a storm-swept mountain.

I quickly placed an arrow through both lungs of the mountain lion and learned what the term "caterwaul" means. The cat pawed the air for a second and then, in seeming slow motion, fought each limb of the tree on her way down. When she hit the ground, she gave a tremendous leap that took her far out over the cliff. Smith laconically commented that she was dead in mid-air as she turned end-over-end and crashed down into a snow bank far below.

I made my way down the mountain to the cat. She was a truly beautiful animal with a thick winter coat of chocolate-brown fur with a pure white face and ears. We finally dragged my trophy into an open place on the mountain for photos.

Then came the slow, painful return in the fierce blizzard. After many hard hours on the mountain, we arrived back at the truck. We took the cat to the mountain lion expert, Gary Power, the local conservation officer. He aged the lion at thirteen years, too old to bear cubs and five years past her prime.

One of her main front teeth was broken off, and she probably had been unable to kill any large game. This was borne out when we checked the claws. Power found that they were worn down from trying to dig out small animals from their dens. The big cat probably wouldn't have made it through the winter.

The skull officially scored 13-1/16, which assured it a berth in the Pope and Young records. After skinning the cat, Gary invited us into his comfortable home to warm up. He then began to narrate the hunt that had culminated in his tagging of the cat I had just taken. He disappeared for a moment into his study and returned with a beautiful photo of my trophy cougar, a photo he had taken the year before when he had tagged her. "Congratulations, Billy," he said, as he gave me the photo. "You've gotten yourself a double trophy!"

"Triple trophy," I announced happily. "Today is also my birthday!"

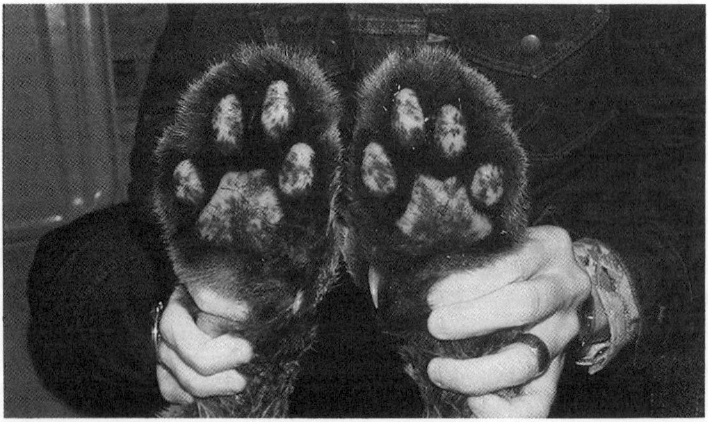

Giant paws of the old cougar

Author with his triple trophy cougar in a fierce blizzard

Gary Power's previous year photo of author's trophy

Bowhunter

In Homage to Robert W. Service
The Bard of the Yukon

Bowhunter, what are you doing here, on the white top-knot
o' the world,
Hugging a smudgy willow fire, deep in a Lynx robe curled.
Where the wind has the cut of a naked knife and the stars
are rapier keen,
Why did you come all the way up here, what does your
madness mean?
Go home to the warmth of your own home fire, and the
feast that waits for you,
Instead of scouring this land of the Northern Lights on the
trail of the Caribou.
Go home to your country club, bowhunter, home to your
evening dress,
Why do you linger all alone in this splendid emptiness?
And you fled afar from the thing called Peace, and you
thought you would find it here,
It's a weary and a dangerous quest, on the track of the
Grizzly Bear.
In the purple tundras vastly spread, the mountains whitely
piled;
They say that the Lord can be found out here in the secret
heart of the wild.
And you know that heart as few men know, and your eyes
are tired but deep.

With woe and pain have you greatly lain, and ached in
abysmal sleep.
With a "something lost" come welling back from the raw,
red dawn of life;
The soul of the Stone Age leaps in you, alert for the ancient
strife.
And if you came to our feast again, with its pomp and glee
and glow,
A mad sun goading to frenzied flame, the glittering gems of
the snow,
I think you would sit stone still, bowhunter, and see in the
daze of a dream,
A monster Musk Ox bulking black, against the blood-red
gleam.
I think you would see berg-battling shores, and stammer
and halt and stare,
At the aching gleam, and the hush of a dream, and the track
of a great White Bear,
With a sudden sense of the frozen void, serene and vast and
still;
And the primal lust that surged in you as you drew to make
your kill.
To feel the pulse of the Silences, and stand elate once more;
To hear again, the Bull Moose call, and the glutted river
roar;
And spy the hosts of Caribou that shadow the shining
plain,
On the verge of the yawning vastitudes that call to you in
vain.
Men soar with wings, and they bridle kings, but what is it
all to you,

For I think you are one with the stars and the sun, and the
wind and your bow so true.
And the peaks untrod that yearn to God, and the valleys
undefiled;
Wise in the ways of the wilderness, and strong with the
strength of the Wild?
You have spent your life in this noble quest, and this hunt
won't be your last;
You have held the throne of the Great Unknown, you have
ruled a kingdom vast!

MUSK OX

Oomingamak the Mighty

The whiteout was almost complete. My snowmobile growled under me like an angry banshee. The Eskimo guides were up ahead, their own snow machines obscured, with only their upper torsos faintly visible. Their heads bobbed up and down in the opaque whiteness like hooded supplicants in a surreal purgatory.

Was this reality or a dream? What ancient urge had driven me to this remote island in the Beaufort Sea, 600 miles above the Arctic Circle and 7,000 miles from the warmth of my hearth and kin?

The lure of the frozen northland is as compelling as it is dangerous, but its animals are some of the most beautiful in the world. The friendly and gregarious Eskimos are attuned to the slightest nuances of nature in order to exist in this demanding environment. Their luxury is survival.

My adventure had started over six years before at the Pope and Young convention in Bismarck, North Dakota, where I had met Joe Fogelman and admired his world record musk ox. As Joe had narrated his epic adventure on Nunivak Island, Alaska, I had vowed then and there that someday I would hunt this interesting and beautiful animal.

In 1979, the government of the Northwest Territories had opened the season for sport hunting of musk ox. The herds were increasing at an alarming rate and needed to be reduced to keep the animals in balance with their food source. There are now between 40,000 and 50,000 musk ox in the Canadian north country, which included Banks Island where I now hunted.

For eight months of the year, the musk ox's range is covered with snow, which he paws up to expose the tender willows, rushes, and sedges that compose the bulk of his diet. For four months of the year, they live in darkness with temperatures averaging thirty-five degrees below zero. Without their remarkably warm two-layered coat, they could not survive. The inside coat is composed of a fine downy wool called "quivit," which Eskimos use to insulate their own clothes, and the outside coat is of strong, shaggy hair that grows over two feet long and hangs almost to the ground. The pelage is choclate brown with a creamy saddle and white stockings at the hooves. A herd bull can weigh up to 850 pounds, and his glory is his white sweeping horns with black tips and a massive "boss" at the top. During the late summer rut, the stillness of the tundra is broken by the crash of these massive horns as the bulls challenge each other for their mating harems.

The only natural enemies of the musk ox are wolves and man, although a polar bear may make off with an occasional calf. Through the millennia, musk ox have developed an effective defense against wolves. The herd draws itself into a circle with the bulls facing out and the cows and calves in the center. While effective against wolves, this is their Achilles' heel when confronting a bowhunter, even though there is a hint of danger as the archer has to go in close to place an arrow. I have seen a bull charge out and chase in circles a guide who was scouting a little too close.

My hunt had been booked through Rick Furniss, an outfitter who represents I.D.C., the Eskimo hunt coordinators. I had flown from Memphis to Inuvik, the last outpost on the mainland of Canada. The I.D.C. hunt package provided fine lodging at the Eskimo Inn, where I met the other hunter, who turned out to be Dr. Brandon Macomber. Brandy is one of the most famous gun hunters in the world, being past president of the Shikar Safari Club and one of the first Weatherby Award winners. His sparkling eyes and excellent physical condition belie the fact that he has seen many hunting seasons come and go.

The chartered King Air flight to Sachs Harbor on Banks Island had been uneventful, although I was bothered when I didn't see any life rafts aboard. Then my guide had explained that they would be totally useless, since a crash victim would only last a few seconds in the icy sea. Sachs Harbor, a village of about 250 inhabitants, was on a lonesome, windswept ridge overlooking the frozen Artic Sea. Brandy and I were boarded in a snug, modular, all-electric house with indoor plumbing and all the comforts of home.

We went out that second day on snowmobiles. It didn't get light enough to see until 10:00 a.m., so we slept late before starting out. My guide was the robust and handsome David Nasogaluak, whose deep booming voice and erect carriage reminded me of a Samurai prince. A mile out of Sachs Harbor, we became enveloped in the whiteout that began this story.

We stopped several times to glass the rare and beautiful Peary Caribou, which is almost pure white and considerably smaller than the other caribou species. David, his brother Eli, and Brandy's guide, Peter Sydney, and I all drove snowmobiles, and Peter pulled Brandy in a kamatik (a wooden cargo sled with metal runners and no shock absorbers). I envied Brandy, snugly covered with caribou robes, until I tried riding one later in the hunt. I would equate this experience with being lashed to a narrow board, hooked behind an Amtrak train, and pulled from Chicago to Memphis at ninety miles an hour.

The whiteouts—driving snow and fierce wind—coupled with the speed of the snowmobile, drove the wind chill factor far below zero and made that first ride difficult, to say the least. The Eskimos had provided snowmobile boots, mittens, and parka, for which I was thankful. After we had traveled about twenty-five miles, the visibility improved somewhat. "We see

The whiteout was almost complete.

Guide David Nasogaluak

Oomingamak soon now," David boomed out over the howling Arctic wind.

A few miles farther on, David stopped and pointed to a distant mountain. There on the snowy foothill was a sight to remember. Eighteen fluffy, chocolate-colored lumps were plodding uphill in the mist and snow. I had come 7,000 miles to see this sight!

In minutes, the guides had put up a snug tent with

caribou robes covering the floor, and had cranked up a Coleman stove and lantern. After hot tea, bannock bread, and semi-raw caribou jerky, David went to check the herd for bulls while the rest of the hunting party waited in relative comfort. An hour later, he roared in with the good news: "Four big bulls! One is very big, and one is tremendous!"

The Eskimos held a brief kitimiort (conference) and, evoking ancient Inuit law, decided that the oldest man would get first shot. We all charged up the hill, and when we broke over the crest of the ridge, the musk oxen drew up their defensive circle far below. Through my Bushnell Banner 8 × 30 roof prisms I saw the biggest bull turn in a circle. Then I heard the boom of Brandy's .458 elephant gun, and saw the animal plop down in the distant snow. Brandy's hunt was over.

At the shot, the herd ran pell-mell over another hill. David and I sneaked up the next ridge to glass the herd. Powerful, high-resolution binoculars like Bushnells are a must in whiteout conditions, and they performed perfectly. We soon picked out the next biggest bull and started toward the herd. As we trudged in closer, they went into their defensive circle again.

As I walked within bow range, I noticed that the old campaigner I had picked had a truly awesome presence about him. His head was down and he was pawing the snow, getting ready to charge. His guard hair rippled in the fierce Arctic gale. His rugged boss showed scars of many battles won and lost. This stately bull had mated while the Northern Lights danced, and I was sure he had sired many offspring that would keep his magnificent genes alive.

He bunched his back legs under him. "He gonna charge anyway!" roared David, breaking my reverie. I quickly drew my sixty-pound Custom Takedown that Fred Bear had signed for me for good luck, and was delighted to see the Dougherty Sunset Smoke 2117 arrow tipped with a Thunderhead 180 take the bull through both lungs. The massive animal lunged at me but quickly collapsed. Jubilation reigned as David put an Eskimo bear hug on me. The bull would later score 106-6/8 Pope and Young points, breaking the old world record by 2/8, but following Ron Koplin's new world record of 108-4/8.

After admiring the animal and taking some pictures, we returned to camp with the bull in the kamatik. In the snug tent later that night, the lantern light bathed the smiling faces of our Iniut guides as they told their sagas of the old days now gone forever. They told of whistling down the Northern Lights, of struggles with the Mighty Whales, of the Great White Bear and their battles with him through the ages, of fellow hunters who had won and of some who had lost.

"Is there a chance we will see a polar bear tomorrow?" I asked.

"Never speak Nanook's name!" warned David. "Last time sport hunter spoke of him, Nanook stuck his head in tent flap!"

I'm here to report I never spoke of Nanook again!

Oomingamak the mighty

Sundogs on the surreal Arctic landscape

MOUNTAIN GOAT

Danger in Paradise

I had left the shelter of a protected ledge to follow my Tahltan Indian guide, Leonard Creyke. We were attempting to side-hill around an extremely difficult slope on the face of an almost vertical mountain in the Cassiar Range in Northern British Columbia.

When I took the first step from hard granite onto rotten shale scree, I knew I was in trouble. I started to slide downhill, gaining momentum. The ultimate conclusion to this little waltz was sliding over the edge of the cliff down below me and then becoming airborne for around one thousand feet. The flight would probably be scenic but the sudden stop would likely destroy any appreciation of it. I did not like this situation at all!

"Run!" screamed Leonard. I ran—Lord, how I ran! I almost made it to firm footing on the other side, but my legs and lungs gave out at the same time; just as my boot touched a tiny bump of firm rock out on the shale slide. I humped up and stopped. I made the mistake of looking down. The small slabs of scree were still dancing down the mountain to disappear into the awful eternity where they seemingly fell forever.

I was now lying on the shifting shale slide with one toe on the miniscule out-crop of firm rock that was mercifully keeping me away from life's greatest riddle.

"You should have kept running," yelled my guide.

"You should insert this mountain in a very uncomfortable place," was my only thought. I dared not yell, as that caused movement, and movement might jar me loose. In a very low, easy breath, I murmured, "Come over and get me." The firm rock was starting to pull out. "COME GET ME, I'M SCEERED!" I screamed. I was now sliding down an inch at a time, but I was picking up momentum. The anchor rock was starting to up-root. My stalwart guide finally realized the seriousness of my predicament and was starting to kick deep steps into the scree. He was slowly backing his way out toward me.

The anchor rock was now almost pushed out of the mountainside when I felt a hunting jacket sleeve slap my face. I grabbed it in a death grip and was soon pulled out of harm's way.

Anyone who thinks Mountain Goat hunting is easy should have undergone *my* ordeal.

We then continued our struggle to the top of the mountain and stopped for a snack. While we were relaxing, Leonard manned the Bushnell Spacemaster spotting scope.

Tahltan Indian guides glassing for goats

"Nice Billy on far mountain," announced my guide. "You wanna go today, eh?" he questioned.

"Nooo way today," I replied, "I've got to replenish some courage before I tackle another goat cliff!"

That night I heard wonderful tales of the great white goat from my loquacious Tahltan guides and wranglers. It seems that for millennia the mountain goat has played a major part in Northwest Indian Culture. The goat was worshipped as an important diety. The goat's meat played a major part in ceremonial dishes and the animal's body parts were fabricated into exquisite works of art. The shiny black horns were fashioned into ritual ladles, jewelry, and ceremonial spear points. The silky white hair was woven into the famous Chilkat blankets and formal attire. The hooves were used for dance rattles and inlay material.

Goat camp in the Cassiars

One of the guides told a tale of the ghostly goat of Iskut. It seems that every time there is a funeral at Iskut, a mystical goat comes out on a ledge overlooking the sacred Indian burial ground. Like an apparition, the goat stands there, imbued with a luminous presence. For untold generations, this goat has provided comfort to these Indians through some mystical, psychic link. At the end of each funeral service, he always vanishes and never reappears until the next burial. Thinking that this was an ancient wives tale, I asked my Tahltan friends when the goat was last seen. "Last week," was the reply!

We next laid our plans for the morrow. The goat was in very rough country but we would try to out-fox him.

The next morning at daylight, we were picking our way upwards, ever higher into the awful rock chutes and towering rotten basalt chimneys. Every toe and finger hold was on loose rock. Several times I made serious resolutions to never get any higher than a tree stand. Finally we topped out to glass for the illusive billy goat.

He was nowhere to be seen. We scanned for hours, but no billy. Finally Leonard broke the silence; "You think billy is on this mountain, you find 'im, eh."

"Is he really out there?" I asked.

"Yea, he's there, eh."

I scanned every nook and cranny with my forty-five power spotting scope, but I never found him.

"You see white dot under the limbs of spruce tree

Author and guide topping-out on a windswept ridge

standing at the bottom of meadow?" he asked. Then I saw him! Just his head, at least a ten inch horn, and a limpid black opaque eye was all I could make out of the bedded billy.

We clattered down a shale slide to the bottom of the wash, went back up the side of the opposite mountain, and prepared to make a stalk. We shucked our packs, tightened our boot laces, and I checked my Bear Grizzly II. All set.

The goat was bedded below us and the wind was in

our face. He was at the base of a tree with a sheer drop-off in front of him. "Noooo problem," I thought.

Our plan was to climb around and over the mountain and come down on the goat from above. Subduing our noise as best we could, we slid down a short scree slope, stalking straight down. We moved into a field of wild flowers so beautiful they would take your breath away. There was alpine azalea, Chukchi primrose, pink plume, wild poppies, and rock jasmine drenching the mountainside with a symphony of fragrance and color. Even on a final stalk, I never have any trouble "considering the lillies of the field."

As we moved close to critical range on our bedded quarry, a piercing "CRUNCH" broke the stillness. I had blundered into a patch of wild celery!

"Look!" rasped Leonard, as he pointed downhill. The possible Pope and Young world record goat was ambling off to our left about forty yards away with an almost astral immunity from harm.

My efforts in getting an arrow off the quiver and on the string were about as futile as the chance of Muhamar Kadhafi winning the Nobel Peace Prize. I was so rattled, I never even *tried* to shoot.

I will always remember that fabulous white ghost of a goat, floating mystically along through the rippling waves of perfumed color. I am certain that the red gods protected that particular goat. He was headed straight for Iskut!

That night around the dancing campfire, the Tahltans told wonderful sagas of their great tribe and I related to them the following tale of an earlier hunt for the Rocky Mountain Goat in the Bob Marshall National Forest in Montana.

Several days into the hunt, our guide Steve Copenhaver, my hunting buddy Joel Smith, and I were picking our way up into goat country. We were on fine mountain horses and had a string of several pack horses to boot. As we wound ever higher above the Copenhaver main base camp on Danaher Creek, the vegetation and the air seemed to get much thinner.

Giant panoramic vistas opened up to us and I could then see why Montana is affectionately known as the "Big Sky Country." Sometimes we were on a well-defined trail and other times we would ride across almost vertical shale slides on ten inch wide Elk trails. Far below, the thundering waterfalls of the South Fork of the Flathead River echoed up to us a chilling reminder of what to expect should a horse slip. At times like this you grit your teeth and like Napoleon's Marshall Ney, mutter "c'est la vie," and toss it all to the wind!

After a grueling all-day ride we neared the goat cliffs that towered above spike camp. Steve had assured us earlier that he had come up here before the goat season and set up a nice wall tent as well as cached some food and provisions for both us and the horses.

As we neared the camp site, we rode down a little dip across a tiny rivulet. "BEAR!" Steve rasped, and jumped off his horse while grabbing his .338 Winchester model 70. He knelt down by a boggy, water-filled basin. The impression in the bottom looked like the track of "Bigfoot," but had giant claw imprints instead of toes. The water was still murky above the track. Ursus Horribilis was here with us now!

"Daddy and I have seen some monsters in here, but this track beats all," whispered Steve. We quickly tied the horses and jacked rounds into our rifles.

We spread out in combat formation and eased in on the spike camp. Closer, ever closer, every rock, every bush, every shadow, is scrutinized, a flicker of brown. . . . ."CRASH, THUNK, THUNK, THUNK, WOOF!" A giant creature was vacating the premises with the finesse of a steam roller.

We stopped for a while to be absolutely certain that the bear had indeed checked out, then eased up to the tent. It was in total shambles. Both sides were shredded and just like the old adage, the bear had gone through the tent "anywhere he wanted to."

The whole camp site was a disaster. Through the bountiful evidence, we pieced together a chilling tale of brute animal power.

The sheep herders' stove had still held some remnants of bacon grease from earlier breakfasts. The bear chewed the heavy iron stove to pieces, while licking the grease. Steve had made a makeshift cache by putting two locked pannier boxes full of canned goods and two fifty pound sacks of horse pellets in a tarp which he then attached to a two-inch-thick hawser rope. The rope was then slung over a high tree limb and the food bag was pulled over twelve feet high in the tree and cinched.

The grizzly was so huge and powerful that he rose to a standing position, reared back, and slapped the tarp bag so hard that the panniers splintered, the thick rope broke, and the whole shebang flew twenty feet from the tree. He walked over to the bag, shredded the tarp, and forced his claws under the heavy steel bands around the boxes. He then pulled his paws up like a wrecking bar and the steel bands popped as easily as a paper cigar band.

He picked up four five-pound cans of peaches one at the time, put each one in his mouth, and crunched down, shredding the sharp tin in the process. He then chewed and sucked out all of the peaches and drank the peach juice mixed with his own blood, because from the sanguine evidence, he had seriously cut his mouth on the razor-sharp tin. He did the same number on all of the other canned goods that were to have been our only source of food for the next five days, with the exception of a few candy bars in our saddle bags.

Next ole Ursus turned to the hundred pounds of horse food, devoured both sacks, and finally took a well-deserved rest. He gradually built himself up to a thunderous finale and then . . . took what must have been the crap of the universe, all over the inside and outside of our tent!

This was obviously one bad, albeit creative, grizzly!

Night fell shortly and we built a bonfire outside the

tent that would rival the famous "burning of Atlanta" scene in *Gone With the Wind.* We ate our meager candy bars for supper, with rifles in laps and fingers on triggers. Unlike the bear, we suppressed any call to go to the bathroom; there were many strange noises out in those bushes; we never slept a wink.

I think during this night there occured a rudimentary call to the ministry for my buddy Joel; a call he would respond to many years later. He also vowed never to hunt outside the Magnolia State again for any critter more dangerous than a possum, and he has always kept that promise.

The chilly dawn found us as bedraggled as dying calves in a thunderstorm. Nobody was in any condition to try for a goat. Opportunity sometimes only knocks once however, so Steve and I gritted our teeth, and decided to fight the goat cliffs. Joel would hunt for mule deer.

For obvious reasons, we didn't leave for Scapegoat Mountain until way after daylight. As we rode out on an open bench to glass, a fine sight greeted us. A plethora of bright white dots littered the foreboding black shale cliffs. Through our spotting scopes they materialized into twenty six nannies and kids. Two big yellow looking lumps off by themselves proved to be fine billy goats.

We plunged down the hill, crossed the churning Flathead River, and tied our horses. Then it was "shanks mare" all the way up that awful escarpment.

Most normal people who live all of their lives at sea

level are afraid of heights; I am no exception: I am *terrified* of heights! I also have, however, a nagging compulsion to climb way up there anyway. My wife is convinced that I am not a normal person. She is probably right.

We were now clutching onto tiny finger and toe holds and were precariously balanced on the cliff face when I looked straight up. "Goat!" I yelled and pointed.

"Shhh, you'll spook it," whispered Steve. The goat ducked out of sight and we cautiously side-hilled to a more stable shooting perch. When we got set, we glassed the terrain, but saw nothing.

Then suddenly, a handsome goat materialized a hundred yards up the cliff. "He's coming our way!" Steve whispered excitedly. The goat hadn't seen or winded us, and it was headed down the same hogback that we were on, obviously going for water far below.

He was truly beautiful, with rakish shiny black horns and big muscles that rippled under that lustrous white coat with each step he took.

The set-up was perfect. The goat was in good range, so I tried to get a good sight picture. "Oh, no! I can't shoot down from this perch at such an extreme angle," I thought.

The goat was getting away. In desperation, I flopped down on my belly, grabbed hold of a gnarled mountain juniper bush with my left hand, and pulled my body out over the lip of the cliff. The cross hairs settled,

The mystic goat of Iskut

"KA-BOOM," and the bush pulled out by the roots from the cliff face due to the awful 7mm recoil. I dropped the rifle, grabbed a rock, and in the nick of time I pushed myself back up on the ledge and prevented my wife from receiving a dandy check from my friendly life insurance agent.

The goat was hit hard but somehow managed to

make it to the skyline where it took a death-dive off the cliff. "The horns will break off!" I groaned to myself. After an agonizing, cliff-hanging, climb down to the goat, I found that my worry was indeed well-founded: the left horn was missing. Thankfully, my diligent guide found the horn after a lengthy search.

My goat was not a monster record book trophy, but it is a wonderful representative of the species, oreamnos Americanus. Atcheson Taxidermy fixed the broken horn and did a half-mount that is a beauty to behold. Everytime I look at that trophy, I have chilling memories of the time that I was almost the hunted instead of the hunter and I recall the visceral fear that I ofttimes feel on the high cliffs.

I also made a vow while clinging to my life with my fingernails and I have always kept it. As soon as I got back home, I sold that blasted 7mm rifle and I have never picked one up since!

Author gets his goat!

MOUNTAIN SHEEP

Meditations on Sheep Hunting

I hate sheep hunting. I hate the agony. I hate being pushed beyond my endurance limit time after time. I hate being wet and sick for days on end. I hate the awful loneliness and the exposure in the presence of fog-clad spires of angry black shale and granite. I hate the interminable bone-jarring horseback rides day after day. I hate the knife-edged, gale-driven sleet. I hate the avalanches and the terrifying abysses. Most of all, I hate the nagging compulsion to go sheep hunting again and again.

But I must and do go back to the land of the frightening loneliness, because I like wild sheep. I like sheep camps. I like the oufitters, guides, and wranglers. I like mountain horses. I like the warmth and smell of a campfire after an assault on the mountain. I like the ecstasy of snuggling into a warm down-filled sleeping bag after a skillet supper of butter-fried medallions of sheep tenderloin. I like the triumphant comraderie between hunter and guide when a sheep slides hooves-up down a rain-slick shale slide.

My Dall sheep hunt was booked with Stan Simpson's Ram Head Outfitters, a first-class operation in the Mackenzie Mountains of the Northwest Territories above the Arctic Circle in Canada. The Northwest Territories' 1.3 million square miles encompass an area larger than Texas, Alaska, California, and New Mexico combined. It is a harsh land of ethereal beauty, with its towering mountains, stark tundra-covered barrenlands, and glaciers and fiords that plane out into great inland lakes and majestic river valleys.

After a flight from Memphis to Edmonton, Alberta, I flew to Norman Wells, my last jumping-off point. Five million barrels of oil lie under this unpretentious village of dirt streets, pre-fab buildings, and friendly folks. I claimed my baggage at the Norman Wells airport terminal building and with five Canadian sheep hunters, boarded a DeHavilland Otter, the Mack truck of the north. We flew 140 miles due west, into the heart of the majestic Mackenzie Mountains, and landed at Stan Simpson's Godlin Lake base camp. Stan's hunting area encompasses over 6,000 square miles. It has produced some of the finest Dall sheep trophies ever recorded.

After a wonderful home-cooked meal at Stan's very comfortable camp, we hit the sack early, with great anticipation of the upcoming hunt. The next day, my guide Richard Heppner, wrangler Sonny Mousseau, and I took four pack horses and made an eighteen-mile

Mackenzie Mountain sheep country

horseback ride in the driving rain out to our spike camp at Wagon Wheel mountain. The following morning, we rode six miles further into the mountains, where Richard and I left Sonny and the horses behind and took off up the mountain on foot, humping our sixty-pound packs.

* * *

Somewhere in the MacKenzie Mountains . . .

I am stranded in our two-man dome tent, having a hard chill here in my wet sleeping bag. It is alternately raining and sleeting a buckshot cacophony on the nylon rain fly. I have a bad respiratory infection and fever, but I'll just have to tough it out. We have ridden and hiked twenty-four miles out here from our main base at Godlin Lake. Still no sheep.

We have struggled up two roaring, boulder-choked streams all the way to the top of the mountain and back, and not a living creature have we seen. We have climbed mile after agonizing mile on foot with our heavy packs, and still no sheep. I am wet, cold, exhausted, and every cell in my freezing body protests this mindless agony called sheep hunting.

My buddies back home, meanwhile, are bow-shooting a cushy animal-round target range in ninety-degree comfort, or riding around in golf carts while stroking a little white dimpled ball, or checking out other forms of dimples by the swimming pool at the Number Two tee. My daddy wanted me to be a golfer. I wish I was right now!

My strong silent sheep guide, Richard Heppner, is walking back to our base camp. Hopefully, in several hours he and the wrangler, Sonny Mousseau, will return with the horses and extricate this battered old banker from this untentable cliff overlooking the raging cataract that we have fought all day. I hear far-off bells that might have been tied on to a sweet chariot and realize that I must have dozed off.

As I struggle back to the land of aching joints and sore feet, I recognize them as the pack horse bells. Richard and Sonny are back, and I have more of this torture to look forward to again tomorrow. The motto up here is: "Are we having fun yet?"

* * *

We got back to our base camp at 9:00 p.m. on July 29th. I felt a little better; my chest didn't hurt quite as bad. Sonny and I rode back with the horses. We left Richard out in the mountains alone. He had gritted his teeth and vowed to find rams; a ram, that weird, unholy grail of broken bodies and shattered dreams. I hoped he would return O.K. I had overheard him tell Sonny if he wasn't back to our base camp by 1:00 a.m., to come looking for him. Then Sonny showed me how to make an emergency call on the radio in case *he* didn't come back.

The mountains can be aesthetically pleasing, but they are also extremely foreboding in reality. Danger lurks around every corner. Sonny and I, on the radio to the main Godlin outfitter's camp, heard Hank, one of the guides on another sheep hunt, call in from the Keel River camp and talk to our outfitter, Stan Simpson.

"Stan, I've got some good news and some bad news!"

"Bad news first," radioed Stan.

"Our boat just overturned in the deep rapids in the gorge!"

"Good news, quick!" Stan called back.

"Good news is we're all alive, but we need clothing and supplies pronto!"

Richard returned about midnight, after a gut-bustin' climb, to dejectedly report "no sheep" again. The next morning, he and I headed back out alone into the mountains with our backpacks. The day started off in agony when we dropped down into a precipitous gorge, with the sixty-pound backpack jamming my knees all the way down to the bottom, and climbed up again to the lip of the gorge on the other side. With lungs bursting, we then side-hilled over the awful boulder fields and shale slides in order to gain about two thousand feet on the mountain. Turning up a roaring mountain stream, we went up and around and over waterfalls, sometimes holding on with toenails and fingernails, before finally gaining the top. We rested in a beautiful grassy basin with shear rock spires like gothic cathedrals towering around us.

"Wrong chute," muttered Richard. My heart sank; I was physically drained. "Let's head back down and try the next mountain."

"No way tonight," I protested. "It's already 8:30." The sun never sets above the Arctic Circle, and time gets away from you.

The next morning, we slept in until 8:30. Then, sore and sick with a chest cold, I followed Richard as he retraced our tortuous route all the way back down so we could punch up another roaring cataract all the way to the top of the next mountain. Richard then left me to R&R while he scouted for the elusive sheep. He returned after several hours. None.

We climbed up waterfalls that would be national monuments in the United States. I was too tired and scared to appreciate them. At times, I would hand my pack up to Richard and then ease myself up and around the sheer, water-slick, black granite cliff faces, using toe and finger holds. We walked up and over glaciers with jagged pieces of flint sticking out of the top like slivers of coal on a snowman's head. We walked through veritable gardens of geologic delights: five million-year-old sponges, shells, anemonies, and coral, frozen for eons in huge boulders and river rocks. No rock-hounding up here, however. By now I could feel the weight of my toothbrush! Once, in the Yukon, when I asked my guide to define a certain rock, he replied, "Leaverite. Leave 'er right there. Too heavy!" A sheep hunt taught me what he meant.

We were in what had once been an ancient sea bed, until God had decided to create some wild sheep habitat and turned the whole she-bang straight up. Eight thousand feet straight up! It increased my faith to be so close to the mountain and feel so wet, cold, vulnerable, and small. I pity the creationists who put man-made finite parameters on God, for He is eternal and far bigger than our tiny transient minds can compre-

hend. (As I write this, out through my dome tent door a gorgeous panorama is unfolding. The sun is peeking through the clouds that far below me are breaking up. They cling with gossamer tendrils to the ominous black shale cliffs like a Japanese Zen painting.)

* * *

I actually made two sheep hunts in one. When we failed to find rams, we made the eighteen-mile ride back to Godlin base. I recuperated somewhat from my chest cold after a few days' rest, and while we were there, our outfitter flew a hunter out to a caribou camp and swept over our hunting area. He found a band of seven rams, two of which were definitely "keepers." So we packed up again and made another grueling horseback ride out to our original spike camp.

The ride left my knees in worse shape than before. We rode the whole day in the pouring rain, and arrived at base camp with spirits to match. After putting up the big wall tent and drying out somewhat, we planned our second assault on the Wagon Wheel sheep mountains.

Since it was light enough to see around the clock here above the Arctic Circle, we never rushed our departure times. We loaded up, saddled up, and pushed off about nine a.m. the next morning. After a two-hour ride, we reined up at the brink of a yawning abyss. Mighty cataracts thundered at the bottom of the gorge. We cinched up our Camp Trails internal frame packs and got ready. Throughout the 'hunt, I had pared my total load from seventy to sixty pounds.

Because of the waterfalls, we had to side-hill over rotten shale for an interminable stretch of mountains. I never looked down, but the rising thunder from hundreds of feet below reminded me of my alternative should a slip occur. We finally traversed the mountain, and met the creek in a more hospitable mood a thousand feet further up the mountain. Pressing on up the creek bed, we climbed up and over a small glacier, and after two hours were almost on top. Ahead was a large boulder field with extreme vertically-pitched slopes on both sides of us.

A strange crackling, booming sound rose above the roar of the waterfalls. It had been raining buckets all day, and lightning had occasionally hit some of the peaks around us. At first, I thought that was what the roar was; then: "Rock slide!" screamed Richard, and we lunged up the mountain to our right. Tons of jagged rocks, from fist-sized stones to giant boulders, cascaded down the mountain and funneled down the narrow gorge we had just come up. I was thankful that we had made it up this far and were on the right side of the creek instead of the left.

The avalanche was over in less than a minute and we renewed our ascent. Suddenly Richard yelled "Rams!" and we both hit the scree. I kept my head down, not daring to look. My guide motioned me up to him. He pointed upward toward a high rock chimney. Four magnificent Dall rams had just come around it and were now gawking across the rock slide.

I thought, "Curosity killed the cat . . . Hmmmmm . . . We shall see about sheep!" When the rams started picking their way back up into the rock chimney, Richard set up his spotting scope and scanned them, now a half-mile straight up the mountain. Through my Bushnell 7 x 26 Custom Compacts, I could tell that two of the rams were immature, but the other two were busters. One had extremely heavy bases but was broomed back to thirty-five inches. The other one was a beauty with large bases, a deep curl with an "argali flare," and both tips intact.

"Good ram," whispered the taciturn Richard.

"Good for the guide, great for the pilgrim!" I thought.

We still had major problems, however. We were pinned down on an open shale slide with no available cover. After a while, the sheep bedded down with their eyes out of our line of sight. Only their horns stuck up into view like huge football helmets.

We quickly planned our attack. Richard manned the Bushnell Spacemaster spotting scope, and at his signal, I was to run full-bore up the mountain in a simian crouch. When the rams stirred into view, he would motion me to hit the mountain. Then, when he had a chance, he would run up to me. In this way we hopscotched up toward the rams. We finally ran out of covering slope.

"Do you think you can climb up that granite cliff by the waterfall?" asked Richard.

"I have to!" I retorted.

"Giver!" he ordered.

A few definitions are in order here. When your guide tells you to "Giver," you are only minutes away from blowing your meager freeze-dried breakfast and are about to totter on the brink of serious coronary and orthopedic problems. If your guide says "Giver s—" (a popular colloquial term for excrement), be prepared for an experience similar to the Bataan death march, the pullback from the Chosin reservoir in Korea, or the march of Field Marshall Von Paulus' German army into the long Siberian night after their capture at Leningrad. You are going to feel like "Crazy" Joey Gallo did after he ate a dozen clams and two dozen machine gun bullets at Umberto's Clam House, and you are going to have the same second thoughts that the scout "Lonesome Charlie" Reynolds must have had when General Custer asked him if he wanted to tag along to check out an innocuous looking Indian village on a gently-flowing stream called the Little Big Horn.

The straight-up climb was a nightmare. Several times I ran out of toe and finger holds, and Richard had to back down the rocky face and extricate me from a fate I'd not like to think about. We finally punched over the top. Richard pressed flat against the rock, the spotting scope to his eye. "Quick!" he whispered as he motioned to me. "Can you crawl up to the patch of tundra above you? You might get a shot from there."

Then started a replay of that universal nightmare, where you try to run from danger, but can't. Everytime I put my toe in the scree, I slid back down. "Hurry!" rasped my disgusted guide. "The rams are getting nervous!"

After a seeming eternity, I made it to the mossy

bench and laid the fore end of "Sweet Thang" (my custom-built 308 Garrett Accur-Light sheep rifle) down and snuggled into what shooting position I could under the circumstances. "What a colorful way to go," I thought, "killing the ram but being kicked into the abyss in the process."

"Shoot the middle ram," whispered Richard. The rams by now had spotted us and were getting nervous, milling around and fidgeting.

I never looked at the wonderful horns. The body of the ram filled all my conscious thoughts. At three hundred yards, they looked like little white mice, even at four power. I settled down, held the crosshairs high on the ram's lung area, and started my squeeze. "Top of the back!" called Richard. I complied, and the rifle barked of its own accord. To this day, I do not remember squeezing the trigger.

The ram flinched. "You got him!" exclaimed Rich, and the ram started to walk out of my life forever. "Maybe not! Shoot again!" he yelled, as I bolted another Federal Premium 165-grain Sierra boattail into the chamber and tried to get another sight picture. The ram took one more step up the rock chimney, quavered, and fell over backward with all four hooves flailing the air. He then started a slow roll that took him a hundred yards down the scree slope toward us. I was too exhausted and emotionally drained to do anything but lay my head down on the rifle and breathe a silent prayer that this thing was basically over.

After a candy bar, we made our way up to the ram. When I got within fifty yards a terrible reality hit me. "I shot the wrong ram!" I screamed to Richard. This was the one that had big bases but no tips. Richard groaned and raced for the ram, grabbing the horns. When he tugged upward, the tips, imbedded eight inches in the black volcanic tuff, triumphantly pointed skyward. Then, and only then, did I come unglued with joy and exultation.

He was an elegant full curl ram, in his prime at nine years of age, and with a horn length of 38 1/2 inches and huge 14-1/2 inch bases which accorded him an SCI

Guide Richard Heppner and wrangler Sonny Mousseau admiring their pilgrim's sheep horns

score of 163-6/8 points and a gold medal. If a "Hallelujah" chorus had suddenly burst out in that starkly beautiful, icy saddle between the peaks, I couldn't have been much more moved.

I guess sheep hunting must be like that old adage about childbirth: the reward of the labor overshadows the pain!

Author and his record book ram

GRIZZLY BEAR

Mixed Bag in Grizzly Gulch

As the DeHavilland Beaver float plane thundered up into the crisp wind, lifting off the Yukon River at Whitehorse, the prop wash whipped two golden eagles off their lofty perch in a gnarled tree at the water's edge. With flared pinions, they flashed by under our wingtip. My dream hunt had begun! Mike Morgan, my hunting companion, and I were outbound 197 miles northwest of Whitehorse to our outfitter Don Marino's base camp. Located at Goz Lake, high in the MacKenzie Mountains, it is the most beautiful and remote piece of real estate left in the hemisphere.

After a round of greetings as we stepped onto the float plane pier at the lake's edge, we stowed our gear in the comfortable wooden-floored tent and repaired to the cookhouse. Over steaming cups of coffee, home-canned preserves, and freshly-baked bread, Don showed us the hunt plan on a topographical map of the area. His plan called for an early start in the morning. We would be supported by Don and his excellent team, composed of guide/wrangler Don Wilson (who was also a B.C. cowboy and ex-rodeo bronco buster), Mike Morgan's guide Melvin White, and a tough young wrangler named Dude Wilder.

After the strategy session, Don set up a bow range, and we put the final tuning on our bows and other equipment. Later on, we adjusted our stirrups and packed most of our gear into the pannier boxes for the long trail ride ahead. I was glad to find that Don had an excellent string of hunting and pack horses, and top quality tack, tents, and other equipment.

This hunt had been years in the making. I had dreamed of a mixed-bag horseback hunt in the Yukon after reading my good friend Fred Bear's *Field Notes* book several years before. Then, three years ago, I had hunted with Don for moose at his camp on Bonnet Plume Lake. Don had an excellent moose area, and I was lucky enough to get an arrow in a very fine Pope and Young record-book moose. Although Don's hunting area was loaded with grizzly, he was only allowed two grizzly permits for his hunters each year. This necessitated booking a mixed-bag hunt, with a grizzly permit, years in advance.

We were hunting near the Arctic Circle, in the "Land of the Midnight Sun." This was a definite hardship on our sleep habits. We spent a restless night, and were up and ready at five the next morning. After a big pancake

Bush plane landing at Goz Lake, Yukon Territory

breakfast, we began our first long day's ride into the prime hunting area.

This remote area of the Yukon was breathtaking in its primal beauty, with jagged peaks rising from tundra-covered benches that plunged down into willow-choked stream beds. A hint of fall was turning some of the high bush blueberry to gold, and they were heavily laden with the delicious purple berries. A young bull caribou stared curiously at us as we passed, and we watched a golden eagle swoop down from high on a shale outcrop and grab a squirrel in its outstretched talons. After about a ten-mile ride, we led the horses and climbed up on a high promentory to glass. Far below, two peregrine falcons circled, their shrill cries wafting up to us on the crisp breeze. The daily cares of the work-a-day world seemed very far away, and the magnificence of this truly wild country was obvious.

"Sheep," mumbled Melvin as he glassed a far-off distinctly-shaped mountain with twin peaks that we immediately named Mount Parton. Through the forty-power Bushnell Spacemaster spotting scope, we could see eight Dall sheep meandering across a distant shale slide. They were too far away for us to tell if they were rams or ewes, but glassing sheep the first day out really got us fired up.

Rain clouds began to gather, and far below we saw the pack train making its way toward our first night's camp site. When we rode in several hours later, a snug camp was set up, a warm campfire was burning, and a fresh pot of thick Yukon coffee was brewed. We sat around the campfire and briefed Don on the sheep-sighting. Tired and saddle sore, we turned in early, with visions of big Dall rams coloring our dreams.

For several days we glassed sheep, but found no rams worthy of a stalk. One day, Don Wilson and I ventured eight miles out from camp to glass for rams. At noon, we rode down to the beautiful Snake River for lunch, and afterward climbed to a high bench overlooking the river. I had just set up my spotting scope when Don exclaimed, "Damn! I left my rifle down by the river!" While he was gone, I lay back on the tundra and drank in the scenery.

There is a timelessness about this land with its great rock outcrops, mighty peaks, and its tundra made up of millions of bracheopods, worts, and lichens. This is also a very fragile ecosystem. The tundra takes ten years to grow one inch, and therefore is slow to heal when disturbed. Earlier, we had passed an ancient Indian burial scaffold that hadn't rotted, and it had been up for at least a century. I became caught up in the rhythms of this land, lying there in the sunshine with a gentle breeze stirring the willows.

I had returned to glassing some Dall ewes and lambs when a strange feeling came over me, not unlike the terror of the deep I had once felt while scuba diving off the coast of the Yucatan. A chill crept down my spine and I broke out in goose bumps. I had the distinct feeling that I was being watched. I wished for a rifle, but, having none, nocked an arrow instead. Slowly I turned around, and saw a slight movement in the scrub willows up the mountain, nothing more.

I was very relieved when Don soon appeared with his rifle, and mounted my sure-footed mare so we could ride up the mountain where I had seen the movement.

There, on top of our in-bound hoofprints, was a smoking-fresh pile of grizzly scat!

"Did you see the bear?" Don asked.

"No, but I felt him!" I shakily replied.

The next morning, Don Marino and I started out early, several hours ahead of the pack train. We rode at a guarded pace, stopping occasionally to glass. We both knew we were in prime grizzly terrain. The Snake River meandered through a wide valley with steep mountains on each side, the wide benches covered with choke berries, blueberries, and ripe crow berries. Chest high scrub willow covered both sides of the river. After riding a couple of miles, Don turned around in the saddle. "Where exactly did you and Wilson see the grizzly sign yesterday?"

I pointed to a spot 200 yards up on a bench to the left. We spurred the horses on and rode for about 100 yards. Suddenly, Don jumped to the ground, grabbing his .458 Winchester Model 70. "Big blond grizzly!" he exclaimed. I quickly followed his lead, looking where he had pointed. Sure enough, partially obscured by the scrub willows along the river, a big blond bear lumbered majestically along.

We hurriedly led the horses a good distance away and prepared for a stalk. I snapped my Quickee Quiver filled with Jim Dougherty XX75 2117 Sunset Smokes onto my sixty-three-pound Bear Grizzly II, and applied some face camo. Don chambered a hot-dog sized .458 cartridge into the open-sighted pre-'64 Model 70 as we silently eased into the chest-high willows. We were ready. We were downwind and a brisk breeze was blowing. Perfect for a stalk.

We soon lost sight of the bear. My heart went into overdrive. One step, stop, look. Two steps, stop, and there was ole *Ursus horribillis*, his long blond hair rippling in the Yukon breeze.

"You go in ahead," whispered Don.

"Do you have a shell in the chamber?" I asked, just to be sure, before moving out ten yards ahead. I saw the grizzly start to feed to our left. I ducked down in a dry wash and ran toward an opening in the willows that I hoped the bear would walk through.

He didn't. He started moving directly toward me, where the willows where too thick to get an arrow through. He was close now—thirty yards. I raised my bow, arrow nocked. The bear came on in to twenty-four steps. As my bow started up, he stood up on his hind legs! He had spotted us! We were eyeball to eyeball!

His chest made a perfect target. A golden aura shone around him in the rising sun. I had the arrow half-way back when with a "woof!" he dropped down into the willows. Was he attacking or retreating? My heart stopped, with death seemingly only a heartbeat away.

Then, like a torpedo wake on the ocean, the bear's path rippled through the willows to our left. My heart sank. The chance of a lifetime was gone, leaving only an occasional glimpse of gold as he raced away through the thick cover. Don handed me the .458 as the bear stood up at a hundred and twenty-five yards for one final look back. "Bust him!" he shouted.

As if the rifle had a mind of its own, the front bead swung across the bear's chest and went off like a clap of thunder. I heard the bullet slap, and saw the bear flip backward. Then all was quiet. The kind of quiet I had only heard in the depths of Mammoth Cave when they turn the lights out.

Don tiptoed up behind me and put his hand on my shoulder. "You done good," was all he said. After the shot, we waited thirty minutes before taking up the blood trail. When we reached the spot where we had seen the grizzly flip over, there was an excellent blood trail, but it led into a stand of almost impenetrable scrub willows, the curse of the North Country.

Don had his trusty Model 70 shouldered and ready as he slowly crept into the willows. "Cover our back trail," he whispered. I backed down the trail with an arrow nocked on my battered old Grizzly II bow. I knew that this was a study in futility, because if the bear circled around and attacked I would never have a chance to even *draw* the bow, much less make a killing shot.

After we had fought our way into the willows for about fifty yards, Don motioned me to stop. He cupped his hand to his ear and silently pointed forward. "Eunnnnuh, eunnnnuh," we could hear the bear's death moan up ahead. We knelt down and peered under the thick branches. Thirty yards in front, the grizzly was crawling toward us, his long claws tearing the willow bushes up by the roots. My guide motioned me to retreat, which we both did with dispatch, I assure you! We waited about ten minutes and when we returned, the mighty *Ursus horribillis* had expired. He was magnificent even in death, his long blond hair rippling in the mountain breeze.

After we skinned the bear, Don took the skin and rubbed it on the horses' noses. They both went absolutely beserk for several minutes, and I was glad they were tied to a tree. I am deathly afraid of horses, and Hugh "Bwana M'zee" Nichols had named me "Tu Hul Hul Sote" many years before in Wyoming. (For those of you not schooled in Nez Percé, that means "Young Man Afraid of his Horses.") We then rode five hours to Don's best Dall sheep area and glassed over a hundred ewes, lambs, and immature rams on the way.

After a much-needed rest, I awoke the next morning with high expectations of taking a fine ram. When I stuck my head out of the tent, however, my hopes were dashed. A heavy fog, which was to continue for five days straight, enveloped the area. About noon it lifted in the valley, and we began to glass for caribou.

A half an hour later, we both detected a slight movement in a deep gorge on the far mountain. Two sizeable caribou racks soon materialized in the fog, revealing just enough to motivate us into trying a stalk. We mounted up and were soon riding down a steep shale slide.

Halfway down, Don's horse suddenly threw up his head, rolled his eyes wildly, and bucked the guide down the mountain. Don grimly held on to the reins, but they broke and his horse stampeeded back over to me and my horse, which reverted to *his* true nature of bucking bronco! I immediately joined Don down on the shale slide with an extremely sore backside, but I somehow managed to hold on to the reins until my horse quieted down.

Don's horse was now in full flight back to camp. Don briefly congratulated me for holding on to my horse as he jumped on and made a mad dash to catch his. We almost had a long walk back to camp. As he left, he also told me that the horses had crossed a hot grizzly track. I spent the next thirty minutes alone, tightly clutching my bow—my only weapon—and looking intently for the bear. I also remembered a similar incident in Wyoming, when my horse had thrown me down a shale slide and Hugh Nichols and his son had rolled around the mountain, chortling insanely and screaming "Rough Rider Rodeo!" Don finally returned with the horses, and we continued our ride toward the caribou.

Crossing the valley we tied our horses right below

Above the timberline—above the clouds

the timberline, climbed the mountain and crawled over to the lip of the ridge. Down below was a magnificent sight. Two SCI gold medal-class caribou bulls were bedded down in the steep draw about five hundred yards away.

We backed off and side-hilled toward the big bulls,

sneaking another peek from a vantage point two hundred yards above them. The biggest one had gotten up and obviously sauntered out of the bottom of the draw, for we never saw him again. The other one was still in the bottom of the draw. I secretly wished for a .270 rifle, but I was determined to try for a shot with a bow. We ducked back out of sight, and by keeping low, ran around the top of the draw until we were in a stalking position above the bull.

I was on my own then, and my heart was beating like a trip-hammer. Fifty yards, forty, and then thirty-five yards above the bull! My Bear Grizzly II came up, I drew, and my arrow was on its way. When the arrow was half-way to the bull, an errant gust of wind kicked the fletching sideways, killing the arrow off. It thunked harmlessly into the tundra mere inches under the bull.

He jumped to his feet, whirled around, and thundered up the draw. As he turned sideways at a full gallop, I loosed another arrow at fifty yards, but the fletching skimmed off the animal's back. Oh, the travails of a bowhunter! Discretion may be the better part of valor, but it will not kill a caribou! Don ran up and I grabbed his 7 × 57 Mauser Mannlicher, quickly pumping four bullets into the bull. None of the shots was a classic quick-kill shot, but their combined effects ruined the bull's day. He was a fine SCI record-class mountain caribou, and I was amazed at the large body size of the animal, also known as the Osborn Caribou.

The intense fog completely ruined our chances for a decent Dall ram, although I did pass up one legal ram hoping for a better one. I still occasionally think about that ram. But the hunt days were running out, and the time finally came to "hit the rigging" for the long two-day ride back to the base camp.

On the first day of the hunt, I had instructed Don to hand me his rifle if we encountered a wolf. A wolf is a creature of perpetual motion and almost impossible to take with a bow. When we had ridden almost five hours, and I was saddle sore, exhausted, and nearly asleep in the saddle, Don suddenly shouted, "Wolf!" and dove off his horse, rifle in hand. I hit the ground running and grabbed the rifle. Don pointed across the scrub willow-choked flat, and I caught a glimpse of silver as the wolf darted through the thick cover.

I ran to the top of a small rise, and the wolf stopped to check us out at a hundred thirty yards. Only his head and neck were visible as I squeezed off a shot. At the boom, the wolf disappeared. After watching for a few seconds and detecting no movement, we trotted to the spot where we had last seen him. There he lay with a shattered spine—silver, buff, black, and beautiful!

"Big wolf," my outfitter noted laconically. I had never seen a wolf that close, so you couldn't prove it by me! What a fabulous way to end a memorable hunt.!

Two weeks later, Hugh Nichols measured both the Caribou and the Wolf and made it official. "Both trophies should win a Safari Club gold medal, Tu Hul Hul," quoth my buddy, "and they should give you a BBL medal also."

"What for?" I asked.

"BLIND BEGINNERS LUCK!!!" Hugh laughed.

Author with his Gold Medal trophy wolf

Gold Medal mountain caribou

Author with his beautifully furred grizzly

Oh how my heart will ever ache;
when memory calls me back again;
to your crystal mountains, azure lakes,
with eagles dancing in the wind.

Credo

I have seen the sun a-rising on a rocky mountain crest,
and felt the aspens shiver in the north wind's chilling blast.
I have hiked across the tundra in its colors red and gold,
and stalked up on a grizzly bear so beautiful and bold.

I've heard the lonesome foghorn of a towboat on the move,
and heard a gobbler answer and my heart would skip a
groove.
At dusk down in the Delta, high in a 'simmon tree,
I've seen a deer snatch his last bite, before my shaft flew
free.

I've been out in a blizzard in the icy Arctic land,
and spied the mighty musk ox, so haughty and so grand;
And seen the gaudy Northern Lights high in the freezing
air,
and watched in awe as they displayed their colors wild and
rare.

And all I have is wonder for these treasures of our land,
for I know they're created by the good Lord's mighty hand,
And I always try to thank Him for what He's given me,
and when I take that last trail, His grace will comfort me.